CROWDANCING

and the

CHEROKEE STORYTELLER'S BAG

K. MARK HILLIARD

A Memoir of My Expanded-Imagination

Editor: Jordan Russ
First Reader: Emily Mae Bergeron
Cover Photo: Emily Mae Bergeron
Cover and Book Design: Whitnee Clinard

Published by
Moloney-O'Brien
A division of The Hilliard Institute
for Educational Wellness and Hilliard Press

Franklin, Tennessee
Abbeyleix, Ireland
Oxfordshire, England

www.hilliardinstitute.com

Crowdancing and the Cherokee Storyteller's Bag

Dr. K. Mark Hilliard

A Memoir of My Expanded-Imagination

moloney ⊗ o'brien

Table of Content

Prologue

"Nothing connects people like a story shared."

The Main Characters

This is a story composed of multiple intriguing tales, each taking place in the middle of the Seventeenth Century (1650s forward).

The main characters and major places of interest include:

- **Crowdancing**: A young half-Irish, half-Cherokee Indian boy of the Long-Hair Clan, along with his Irish and Cherokee family and their mysterious heritage;

- **Crowdancing's Father**: An Irishman with a strong cultural connection with the O'Mores of Ireland, The Rock of Dunamase, and the Slieve Bloom Mountains.

- **Crowdancing's Mother**: A Cherokee woman with deep roots in the mountains of North Carolina and the surrounding states.

- **The Storyteller**: An ancient and immortal Cherokee Indian Storyteller and his enchanted Storyteller's Bag;

- **Kituwa** [ga-Du-wa]: The very real and ancient Mother-Town of the Cherokee people in the mountains of North Carolina.

- **The Close-One**s: Crowdancing's group of closest friends with whom he has many grand and mystical adventures in his days-of-youth;

- **The Village-of-Angelica in the Valley-of-Elk**: A hidden land in the East Tennessee Mountains in a place now called Jellico; a magical and sacred community of Scottish, Irish, Cherokee, English, and people with various shades of dark skin; a place of youthful and innocent romance;

- **He-Who-Knows-Most**: A Cherokee wizard from the Red-Paint Clan, who is charged with training Crowdancing on his pathway toward becoming a medicine-man;

- **Cherokee and Irish Enchanted Crows**; and

- **Cherokee and Irish Little-People and Faerie-Folk.**

A Personal Memoir:

This book is a personal memoir in that it covers portions of my real-life and imaginative-life from before I was born to about age fifteen—all blended together within authentic Cherokee and Irish history, legend, and lore. The actual dates of my personal involvement with the storied-events took place in the 1900s. But I have transposed, or transported, each of these dates back to the same dates in the 1600s.

For example: I was born December 7, 1957. But in the story, as Crowdancing, I was born on December 7, 1657. And other important timelines of my life are likewise transported back to those dates in the 1600s, each corresponding with the same dates in the 1900s.

Prologue

A Meta-Narrative:

Based on my personal definition, I would consider this book to be
a meta-narrative in that it uses stories within a story, tales within
a tale, and narratives within a narrative to convey a united story of
the early life of Crowdancing and the Cherokee people. These stories and tales and narratives are based on my very-individualized
interpretation of actual historic information; my extensive ritu-
alistic experiences with Cherokee and Irish culture; my graduate
and post-graduate academic research and training into sensory
teaching and learning, the expanded-imagination, enchantment,
and sacred-space; and the personal meaning I have discovered in
my individual pursuit and pondering of each.

These stories all come together in what the Cherokee called a
Bundle-of-Talk, as they are drawn from the Cherokee Storyteller's
Bag. These stories take place in the Land-of-Blue-Haze—the Great
Smoky Mountains of North Carolina and Tennessee—beginning
in the most ancient village of the Cherokee Indian people. Though
the places within each story may look much different in the twen-
ty-first century than they did at the time of each story, most can
still be visited today. As for the key characters, they are all based
on real friendships as well—a composite of people who had special
meaning in my days-of-youth.

The Expanded-Imagination—A Journey Into the Enchanted:

This then moves the story into the expanded-imagination aspect
of the memoir. Our expanded-imagination is activated when our
mind and spirit join together as they experience enchantment
through sensory stimulation.

Much too often we wait for enchantment in the big things.
We wait for our teens, adulthood, college, marriage, a perfect
job, a vacation, then retirement . . . Or, we might simply push

enchantment totally out of our life as we grow into adulthood
or move closer toward any of these new life experiences. We let
enchantment disappear, or pass us by as our life-pages are turned.

Yet authentic enchantment, this journey into our expanded-imagination, is meant to be something we experience every single day of
our lives, at every turn, and at every age.

Our expanded-imagination takes us to that place where we push
a bit of reality outside the lines, and we take a bit of enchantment
and pull it inside. Not so much that people think we are senile. But
maybe enough to make them wonder! The expanded-imagination
is not meant to displace reason, but it is meant to enchantedly
compliment it.

This enchantment of the expanded-imagination takes place when:

1. Our mind joins with our spirit,

2. Our conscience joins with our heart, and

3. Our body joins with our soul.

And then, our spirit and soul are asked to come out and play!

I find this usually happens, or at least begins, through ordinary
sensory stimulation. Through my years of doctoral and post-doctoral research into sensory teaching and learning, I have come to
understand that each of our five senses is meant to be a conduit to
a higher-level, or higher-degree, of sensory experience.

We begin with one of our senses, but with pratice, we
can learn to move beyond the physical and reach into our
expanded-imagination.

Prologue

In simple language, we learn how to see, hear, touch, taste, and smell with our spirit and soul! This is the world of the expanded-imagination.

As a general rule, someone, something, or many things trigger various sensory-stimulation-detectors in our body through smells, flavors, sounds, visuals, textures, forms, feelings, and emotions—and then they request a response. They always request a response!

Yet, again and again . . . we fail to respond.

Maybe we briefly laugh at something humorous, or we smile at something that momentarily pleases us, or we may even say, "Yes, I will do that someday." But then we go about our business as usual and our opportunity to join with our expanded-imagination through sensory enchantment slips us by.

On the other end of various sensory phenomena are those situations where we are so bombarded by sensory stimulation that we experience sensory-overload, and in that state of over-stimulation, what might have offered great joy and meaning offers nothing but aggravation and stress.

In my last book, *The Crow's Enchanted Dance*, I note "Enchantment offers an exquisite agitation of the senses with both brief and extended moments of the purest delight." Yet, as we age, we often begin to see these exquisite agitations as negative, or burdensome, or unnecessary, rather than as delight. This seems to me to be an incredibly inappropriate response by our mind and body in which we are tricked into thinking that this mundanity is how life is supposed to be lived.

In my effort to show you, the reader, how to bring your senses into contact with your spirit and soul—in your expanded-imagination—this first book of the *Crowdancing Trilogy* provides examples through the means of stories—stories that merge together various parts of my real life, imbedded into, and influenced by, the authentic realm of Cherokee and Irish legend and lore and truth. It is a journey into the mysterious realms of thin-space, sacred-place, and sacred-space in a world I have coined The-Space-That-Flows-Between—the only place where the expanded-imagination can truly thrive. This Space-That-Flows-Between is a place of enchantment where the spirit and soul are *not-only-allowed, but-are-encouraged* to come out and play.

Once you have finished reading these stories, I ask you to further activate your own expanded-imagination by taking any sensory stimulation and following it deeper, higher, or further to find its source, its purpose, its essence. Then, as a writer, write!

For example: You smell something in the air. Go out and find the location of the smell, take a photography and study what it is and why it smells like it smells—this activates the expanded-imagination because you are getting to the essence of the smell. Then try this with each of the senses. You see something red in the distance . . . You hear a bird's call . . . etc. This is your assignment for this coming week!

Cherokee Storytelling:
The Bundle-of-Talk Kept Within the Storyteller's Bag

Much of the early history of Native Americans—Indians, as the Cherokee call themselves—and how tribes lived and worked and played and believed has been lost. The earliest records of various tribes were passed down generation to generation through oral stories, traditions, rituals, and drawings kept on leather skins; marked on cave walls and other stone drawings; or placed (stored) through storied-memory in a piece of cloth, a stone, a feather, or

Prologue

any object composed of matter and kept in a sacred-place—such as
the Storyteller's Bag within this story.

These early narratives were not written down with common words
until outsiders came along and recovered traditional stories from
the *old-ones* who were still living—stories told to them by the
ancient-ones of days-long-gone; or when a tribe learned their own
way to write their stories with their own union of symbols into
unique cultural words and language.

Sequoyah [Se-Quo-Yah] in 1821 was one of the first to create such
an Indian written tribal language for the Cherokee, along with
its own unique alphabetical letters; and this language is still used
to this day by the Cherokee people. This ambitious achievement
finally made reading and writing, as we think of these processes
today, possible for the Cherokee. Written stories, before this
time, were created by those who lived with the Cherokee and
wrote down the stories they were told, and shared the details
about the ceremonies they observed or took part in. And through
my research, I determined what was shared was not always what
was true. Sometimes, what was shared was actually a way of
hiding what was true as a means of self-preservation or based on
cultural-sacred-principle.

One thing you will find in a study of ancient Cherokee culture is
that they have always viewed language as a divine gift, whether
in words, stories, drawings, or storied-memory. And this book is
collected from all four of these methods of shared history, with a
narrated emphasis on stories as shared from an ancient Cherokee
Storyteller's Bundle-of-Talk, kept deep within his Storyteller's Bag.

Before they had a written language, it is documented that the
Cherokee used a lot of superlatives in the way they talked—the
most, the best, the crow is smarter than the blackbird, etc. They
also used less pronouns than typically used in modern day language

style, and frequently configured their own unique phrases—I have
left, I went and saw, I spoke the speech, etc. And they loved double
statements—I do not lie, I tell the truth. You will find this language
throughout this book, in my attempt to recapture the original
voice of the story as it might have been spoken in the 1600s.

You will also find traditional Cherokee-type-phrases separated
by dashes, such as Bundle-of-Talk, The-One-Who-Cures-People,
The-Place-Where-We-Stand, etc. With each of these phrases-with-
dashes, there is meant to be very-tight-unity, a-pulling-together
of words by joining them together with dashes. If they are capi-
talized, they are likely more formal titles (as noted above), with
uncapped-dashed-phrases being less formal or one-offs. And
sometimes, I just went with what felt right with a specific phrase,
within a specific context, throwing caution and consistency to the
wind.

History and film often portray the Cherokee Indians as sim-
ple-minded, only able to put together a few words at a time.
However, in reality they often used very elaborate superlatives and
rhetoric—a style of speaking that can turn very poetic and persua-
sive when heard aloud. And their stories, their talk, their speeches
had a strong passion, a feel of poetry and rhythm, but without
the conventional rhyme you often see in traditional poetry. Their
speech was not to a set-measure, nor with an exact-number or
strict-rhythm, but it had a very poetic flow still the same.

To my delighted-surprise, I also found that the Cherokee of the
time period for this story often used their speech patterns like the
words written for a song or psalm, or hymn or prayer; so reading
this story aloud—either audibly or at least with a aloud-emphasis
within your head—will help the reader get a better feel for this
intended rhythmic style. And the very layout of the text itself into
a psalm or poem style format is meant to help with this read-aloud
process. In preparation for this story, I actually read aloud and

studied the entire one hundred and fifty psalms multiple times over the period of one year—one or two psalms every day.

Cherokee Real-Aloud-Style-Format for the Text

To help you better utilize and understand the olden-day Cherokee speech pattern style used in writing this story, I have provided several examples of the process below.

For example, if a sentence is broken into multiple lines that end with commas, there are obvious breaks or pauses as you read, with an intended breath or half-breath after each comma.

Just below the counsel house and sacred mount, (breath)
laid a village-square smoothed flat with human toil, (breath)
and covered thin with sand.

If a sentence is broken with commas within one line, they are meant to have a small pause, with an emphasis on each key word (dances, festivals, ceremonies, games), but a full-breath is not necessary.

*The **dances**, the **festivals**, the **ceremonies**, the **games**.*

And if a sentence is broken into lines that do not end with commas, and the following lines are indented, read through them without a break or pause—like a long-held note on a musical instrument, or at least as much as possible. With some very long sentences that have no commas (as below), you may need to take a gentle but quiet breath, but with no emphasized pause. Rather, place that emphasis on each key word (mud, grass, thatch, bark, plants, trees).

Cherokee History

The early recorded written history about the Cherokee, to which we have access, came in small journaled accounts made by a few explorers in the 1400s and 1500s, and was very, very sparse. Almost nothing was written about this tribe in the 1600s. Then starting in the early 1700s, we began to have written stories about the Cherokee, but once again these stories were written by outside explorers living among the Cherokee for periods of time, and not written by the Cherokee themselves. It wasn't until the 1800s, after Sequoyah created the written Cherokee language, that we began to have history accounts written by the Cherokee themselves.

What I have done in this story about Crowdancing and the Cherokee is put together two ends of early-written documented history (the 1400s and the 1700s forward) with the period of time that falls in between created via speculative-historic-fiction about what was likely going on during the 1600s, based on the time periods before and after.

Within this expanded time-period, and even as I looked further back in time, I determined there was a strong probability of a people living among the Cherokee within the mountain regions that are a part of this story who were of Scottish, Irish, and English decent; a dark-skinned people likely from Africa; a mixed-dark-skinned race of people of unknown origin; and others. This diverse mix of cultures had ventured into these areas as early as the seventh century, or at least by the eleventh or twelfth century.

Prologue

Along with their culture, they brought with them their myths, stories, songs, singing styles, musical instruments, clothes-making techniques and equipment, farming processes, and even building styles. Some of the things we think of as being "invented" in the 1800s, or later, were actually in use at a much, much earlier time—not always in their final patented-form, but still functioning in much the same manner as they would one day take or become better know.

There is also strong speculation that the people from Ireland were perhaps the first to share a Judeo-Christian message with Native American tribes living throughout what would become known as the Americas, including the Cherokee—though some Cherokee would say they were the first ones to come from the Creator, and that they learned what they know of the Creator directly from Ye-HO-Waah, a name they were using for the Creator sometime before the beginning of the 1700s.

Some of these thoughts have stimulated extended studies into a possible Hebrew line of decent for the Cherokee (with pros and cons on each side of the argument); early Judeo-Christian intermarriage with the Cherokee; or an expansion of the Judeo-Christian message to the American Indians by monks, ministers, and missionaries much earlier than some historians suspect. One definitive finding of my studies into the Cherokee, the Irish, and the Judeo-Christian legacy found within each is that newly founded Christian settlements, whether in Ireland or the Americas or elsewhere, would often layer their communities atop old pagan or mythological sites and rededicate them to Yahweh—The Creator God of the Bible. Or, pagan sites would layer their newly founded communities atop old Christian or Jewish sites and rededicate them appropriately. These types of multi-layered archeological sites are still being uncovered throughout the world all the time. And little by little, these sites tell us a bit more of the history they hold within their layers, all waiting to be uncovered. This brings all new possibilities of pondering for the expanded-imagination.

With all this in mind, this story and its many tales is full of accurate historical facts and myths, and truly authentic places and events, along with an element of fantasy and mystery anchored in historical, mythological narratives, all told by an ancient Cherokee Storyteller. A storyteller who has a unique and mystical tie to the lead character within the trilogy—Crowdancing. This relationship develops and is uncovered more and more as each tale moves forward.

As the researcher and writer for, and subject of, this memoir of my expanded-imagination, I offer detailed factual information when it is available and provide speculative-imaginative answers in places where there is little authenticated history to be found. I invite you to not simply come along for the ride, but to enter each tale as a character, your own character—perhaps as a spirit-animal seeing and hearing everything as it is being shared by the Storyteller for the first time—or as a traveling companion with Crowdancing, maybe as one of the Faerie-Folk or Little-People.

In closing, I ask you to try to utilize your own expanded-imagination, to encounter mine.

Stay enchanted,

Dr. K. Mark Hilliard (Markus Crowdancing Hilliard)

Prologue

Chapter One: The Beginning

"When you think it is the ending, perhaps it is simply a fresh start to an old beginning."

December 6, 1657–The Storyteller:

It had been an unrelenting winter thus far,
and what seemed like a plentiful supply
    of wood cut for the fire,
back only the span of two full moons,
was almost gone;
any wild berries left on the vines from the late summer,
were buried under a thick layer of snow;
and any wild game for food,
was unusually scarce.

The land of the Cherokee is beautiful in the fall and spring,
and even in the winter;

but this season was abnormally harsh,
and The-One-Who-Is-Born-at-Night was alone.
Alone except for her little one of only three years,
and another to be born at any time.

The One-Who-Cures-People—
the priest, the conjurer, the medicine man,
had told her not to have any more children,
but this she did not hear.
Her first had been very difficult to jump-down,
but once he was here,
she already knew she would have two more.
For she felt in her heart that each had some gift to share,
even before they were born.

The-One-Who-Is-Born-at-Night's husband
    had been gone from home for some forty days,
in search of food;
and not yet a word.
Each Cherokee village had its messengers—
those who ran from place to place
    sharing any news of importance,
but *of* The-One-Who-Is-Born-at-Night's husband . . .
there was no news.

He was only to have been away for a few days,
at the most,
and his wife was anxious and filled with fear.
She was afraid of loss,
of being a mother alone;
yet she did not wish to think . . .
on what she would do . . .
if the one she loved did not return.

Chapter One

Their cabin was but a day's walk
    to the Cherokee Mother-Town
—Kituwa [ga-Du-wa]—
a walk she could make in half that time
    when not with child,
and there she could find One-Who-Helps-With-Birth—
a mid-wife.
But with the piercing wind and icy snow,
with the darkness of night fast approaching,
and a new baby who would come at any time,
she would not try that journey to make.

On this night,
the woman lay with her child by her side,
and a restless sense of alarm;
alarm mixed with unexplained enchantment
    deep within her soul.
And she sang!
She sang a tune of old that her husband had taught her;
a rhythmic song in the style of *his* native home of Ireland,
with each note gently gliding up and down . . .
down and up.
"If I call your name,
would you come to me;
if you hear my call,
could my face you see?"

And finally . . . she slept.
She slept knowing deep within her heart
    that mystery was so very close at hand;
an allure she could not explain.
Something new was so near she could almost
    hear it, see it, feel it.
It was like a curtain,
waiting to be drawn back,
from the very air she breathed.

"O-E-A . . . Yah!
What I have said is true.
And I, the Storyteller, do tell this tale."

Chapter One

Chapter Two:
A New Day

"Enchantment is just outside your cabin door."

December 7, 1657, 8:59 a.m.–The Storyteller:

On the cold winter day that Crowdancing was born,
his mother awoke to the sound of crows,
dancing crows of three,
just outside her cabin door.

This was not the common raspy sound
    that crows most often make—
with their sharp pitched and loud
    "CAW! CAW! CAW!"

It was a gentle cry of soft and pleading emotion
—of coos and rattles and clicks—

kraaa . . . kraaa . . . kraa.”
A mystical sound carried by the wind
    through the very walls of her home—
“listen to me . . . listen to me . . . listen well.”

It was the sound only made by enchanted crows
    as they summon someone into their mystical realm.
This music,
heard only by this mother-to-be on this magical day,
was a hidden mystery,
but one that was soon to be revealed.

To understand this mystery,
I, the Storyteller, must tell—
there are crows-who-are-common,
and there are Crows-Who-Are-Enchanted.

Common crows are the ones seen all about the village,
or as you walk the woods, most any day.
But these crows,
the crows outside this expectant mother’s home,
were of the latter kind—
they were enchanted!
And enchanted crows are like none other.

Though they *may be seen* among the common crows,
they will often pull away to themselves,
or in pairs of two or perhaps three,
and dance and shake atop a tree,
beside the entrance to a trail,
on the post of a fence,
in the middle of an open field,
or just outside a cabin door!

Chapter Two

And if it is the-most-special-of-needs,
you may, perhaps,
see a White-Crow—the most enchanted of all;
who only makes his presence known
        as a guide through and to a mystical place
        that confuses both time and space.

These enchanted crows,
of any shade,
of black or white or mix of both,
are Bringers-of-Magic;
guardians of The-Space-That-Is-Thin;
gatekeepers of Places-for-Enchantment;
messengers between The-Space-Through-the-Clouds
        and The-Place-Where-We-Stand,
in the overlapping Space-That-Flows-Between—
that uninterrupted space that is sacred,
since the beginning of time.

This call . . .
on this magical, mystical morning . . .
was an invitation into The-Space-That-Flows-Between.
A place where authentic magic finds its home.
A place where beyond-your-wildest-dreams
        becomes a reality.
A place that cannot be explained with ordinary words
        or with simple artless thoughts,
or modest lucid dreams.

As The-One-Who-Is-Born-at-Night listened
        to this ancient mystic-call,
she closed her eyes and breathed in the sound.

This was not a simple breath through nose and mouth;
she breathed in with eyes and ears with fingers and toes

with arms and legs.
She breathed in all that surrounded her,
with all that was within her.

Slowly, and gently,
she then began to release her breath—
into the twirling, twisting lights
    that swam just beneath the lids of her eyes.
And ever so quietly . . .
she slipped through the Thin-Space that surrounded her,
into The-Space-That-Flows-Between.

There, in this space of safety,
this space of peaceful warmth and joy,
this space that had allured her spirit
    the very night before,
she gave birth to a beautiful baby boy
    and gave him the name . . . Crowdancing!

At the very moment of birth,
The-One-Who-Is-Born-at-Night's husband returned.

He walked through their cabin door
    with no knowledge of where he had been,
or that he had been gone for so long a time;
but in his hands were a bundle of fresh berries
    and the meat from an elk already skinned, dressed,
and ready for the fire.

The only memory of his travels was that he was lost,
when he encountered a White-Crow,
and followed his pleading kraaas
    out of the mountains.

Chapter Two

Then, as if it were only a moment in time,
the man was back at his home,
with these gifts of berries and meat;
no knowledge from where they, or he, had come.

As Crowdancing's mother placed the new boy
    into his father arms,
their other son holding tightly to his legs,
the sun began to shine
    out from under the heavy clouds,
the fierce wind became still,
and the tiers of snow laid thick upon their roof,
and packed tall upon the land that surrounded their home,
began to fade.

And there,
just outside their cabin door,
stood a freshly stacked pile of seasoned wood,
cut and ready to burn.

The cool, fresh air
    smelled of wild spearmint and berry-cider.
You could taste it in the breeze,
though there was no seeing
    from where the scent came.

A billowing spiral of gray smoke was soon pouring
    from the open chimney in the centre of the home.
And the house,
for the first time in weeks,
was warm;
the heat attaching itself to the woven sapling poles,
to the plastered mud walls,
and to the upward standing beams
    of long-dried sassafras.

You could feel and smell the tonic of tea, heat, and wood,
as it utterly, and wholly,
consumed the space.

Though none yet understood,
the mystery had begun.
And this . . . that story is.
The tale of Crowdancing,
and the Cherokee Storyteller's Bag.

"O-E-A . . . Yah!
What I have said is true.
And I, the Storyteller, do tell this tale."

Chapter Two

Chapter Three:
The Journey Begins

*"A myth is often much more than an enchanted tale;
it is the story one holds-within,
until someone pulls-it-out."*

Between Time and Space—The Storyteller:

Some say the lore of Crowdancing is simply a myth—
a mere enchanted tale.
But I, the Storyteller, have travelled with him
    in his youthful days of fun and folly,
and on his countless grand adventures beyond.
And I know the words I speak,
are far greater than any fable.

These tales will take you on a journey;
a journey to the ancient Mother-Town of the Cherokee;

to the ceremony at which Crowdancing
    received his forever name;
to his youthful deeds and his days of play;
to his grand adventures with those he called Close-Ones;
to the beginning days of innocent romance;
and to *that-day . . . that-day* that changed everything!

Crowdancing's story will take you into
    the midst of ancient Cherokee ceremonies;
into the enchanted lands of faerie and fae and dragon and crow;
into the hiding places of the Little-People of the Cherokee;
into the homes of the Faerie-Folk of Ireland,
and near and far beyond.

These stories will take you into an enchanted world
    of unseen realms on earth and realms afar;
into the lives of *The-Cherokee-Real-People,*
and their real-places;
places that once stood within time itself,
and some still do;
yet by some magical mystical means,
these places now transcend both time and space,
and the hearer of these stories,
along with them.

But that-is-enough … for now!
Let me begin my first tale.
I will pull it from my Bundle-of-Talk;
I will draw it from deep within the Storyteller's Bag—
the Storyteller's Bag in which all of
    Crowdancing's stories are held captive,
only to be released as the stories are told.

Chapter Three

"O-E-A . . . Yah!
What I have said is true.
And I, the Storyteller, do tell this tale."

Chapter Four:
Crowdancing's Ancestry The Homeland of Ireland— The Hill-Dwellers

*"Before there was me,
there was you,
and Ireland was your home."*

Dedicated to my father, Emerson Jasper Hilliard—Seaspar

Before Time and Throughout Time—The Storyteller:

To understand the mystery that is Crowdancing,
you must first spend a day with his ancestors.
For without their stories,
Crowdancing's story does not exist.

Crowdancing's father was Seaspar [SHAS-per]—
The-Wise-One.
He was an Irishman through and through.
Seaspar was a holy man
    from the Midlands of Eireann [Ireland];
the county of Laois [Leash];
the Queen's County;
the Land of the Monks;
in the Provence of Leinster—
these are some of the many names
    this land would one day take,
some names . . . they already have.

Laois is a beautiful emerald land,
not because of its water,
for its streams are the color of Irish whiskey
—and just as good to drink—
but it is an emerald land
    because of the brilliant color of its fields of grass.
A beautiful garden planted deep in the heart of Ireland.

Though no ocean touches its green meadows,
the ocean's breeze can always be felt in the wind,
and seen in the swaying movements of its leas of grass.
A movement that appears as a twin sister
    to the waves of the ageless sea.
An eternal energy passing through Ireland's fields,
just as it does her seas.

Seaspar's family at one time made their home high upon
    the grandest Rock of Laois;
the Rock of Dunamase [Dun-a-MASC];

Chapter Four

once the stronghold and centre of learning for the
    mighty clan O'Mordha—the O'Mores [o-MOREs],
with whom his clan had bravely served.

The Rock is a place where the winds eternally rage,
and the Irish crows can be seen in meandered-flight,
as the winded-gales forever toss them about.
It is a place of excessive beauty and rugged power;
a place from where you can see . . .
as far as you can see . . .
and just a bit beyond.
I have stood upon this grand rock
    and gazed upon the land beyond its fortress.
There, with Crowdancing at my side,
we have conferred of our days of past adventure,
and planned for days ahead.

From this mighty rock the ancient world,
From-Creation-and-Soon-Thereafter,
can be entered.
Entered at the place where Crowdancing and I have stood,
as others there before us,
and the place where more will stand,
in The-Land-of-Days-to-Come.

It is here among the ruins of Dunamase,
layered atop an ancient Christian settlement,
that the Mightiest-of-Magic waves her wondrous wand.

The Rock of Dunamase is a sanctuary like none-other.
It is A-Place-for-Enchantment
    that time and matter *cannot* contain.
A place where one can enter
    The-Space-That-Flows-Between,
with just the gentlest of tugs by the enchantment

that abounds at every turn,
in every stone,
in every flower growing outward from every stone,
and by the very footprints
    deeply embedded in the thickly stor-ied soil—
footprints placed there by all who have gone before,
and somehow,
by those yet to come.

As far back as there is uttered Irish tales-to-tell,
Crowdancing's father's family were spirit-guides
    and peacemakers;
teachers, writers, priests, and monks.
And caretakers
    of the lands of Laois amongst the O'Mores—
a noble family
    of poets and writers and teachers themselves.
But unlike the Hill-Dwellers,
The O'Mores were also a clan of grand and fierce warriors.

It is said that after the O'Mores
    were vanquished to the coast of Kerry
    by their English invaders—the years of 1608, 1609,
that Seaspar's ancestors stayed behind and
    hid-out in the Mountains of Slieve Bloom,
a land of gently rolling hills
    cloaked in mystery, wonder, and delight.

These are the oldest mountains
    in The-Land-Where-the-Sun-Sets [Europe].
And there—it is said,
Crowdancing's family can still be found today.

Most speak of the ancestors and descendants
    of Crowdancing's father's family

Chapter Four

—those who came before and those who came after—
as the Hill-Dwellers, Hill-Yards, or Hill-Garths,
for they lived within and atop the ancient strongholds,
the fortresses, the mountains, the mounds,
and hills of Ireland.

There, high upon a hill or stronghold,
in open-yards or grounds or gardens,
often surrounded by tall stone walls
    and cloistered hallways,
they oversaw the spiritual well-being
    of the inner sanctum—
the sacred-place that opens
    to the sacred-space,
within which,
the inhabitants of each clan or group of clans gathered to
    learn as they also sheltered themselves from the intrusions
    of the outside world.

Some say the Hill-Dwellers have been in Ireland
    for a mere five hundred years,
but if you ask an Irishman of Laois,
he will tell you,

"De 'ill-dwellers,'ave always been in Ireland.
Dey are a part ov de land itself."

Though known by all,
the Hill-Dwellers are seldom seen in Days-of-Now,
and when they are . . .
it is said to be more like the wind taking shape;
or dancing lights of cloud-like energy
    moving about in the forest;
or a small twisting, twirling stream of water

taking form in the air,
then fastly fading away.

Some say the Hill-Dwellers are the emotions of nature,
emotions that assume visual form,
and thus they are often mistaken as faery and fae.
But I know this notion is falsely formed
    simply because the Hill-Dwellers
    have long made their home
    among the Faerie-Folk of these mountains;
and not because the Hill-Dwellers
    are Faerie-Folk themselves.
For the Hill-Dwellers are of an energy source
    of a different kind than faerie and fae.
It is a forever form.
Their ancient ones have become The-Immortal-Ones.
Their energy . . . is of-the-soul.

Most often the Hill-Dwellers are discerned,
not by their visual image
—though that they just may have—
but by their movements and their sounds,
which are not the common sounds of the woods,
nor the common words used by the local clans.
These sounds are more like an echo
    of ancient Gaelic syllables distorted by the wind.

Once you make the acquaintance of the Hill-Dwellers
—whether by sight or sound or movement or emotions
    felt within—
you will know,
from then forward,
when you are in their midst.
For something stirs deep within each soul,
when you enter into their sacred-space.

Chapter Four

"O-E-A . . . Yah!
What I have said is true.
And I, the Storyteller, do tell this tale."

CHAPTER FIVE:

Crowdancing's Ancestry
The Homeland of Kituwa—
The Cartiers of the Cherokee

"And the two became one flesh, and I became One."

Dedicated to my mother, Lola Bell Carter Hilliard—
The-One-Who-Is-Born-at-Night

Before Time and Throughout Time—The Storyteller:

Though Crowdancing's father was of Irish birth,
his mother—The-One-Who-Is-Born-at-Night,
was a beloved-woman of the Tsalagi [Zah-la-GEE];
The-Principal-People—Aniyunwiya [Ah-knee-YAH-wee-YA];
The-Ones-Who-Live-in-the-Mountains-and-Caves;

The-Ones-Who-Speak-a-Different-Language;
The-Real-People—the Cherokee [CHAIR-uh-kee].

Crowdancing's mother was of the Long-Hair clan—
The Wind, The Twisters;
Those-From-Whom-the-Peace-Chiefs-Come;
Those-From-Whom-the-Priests Come;
And the great Medicine-Men of the Cherokee Indian.

Though some say the Cherokee came here from another land,
the Cherokee say they have always been
    in these mountains,
and they have *always* been Indian.

"Indian is not a name
    the one called Kuh-Luhm-Buhs gave-to-us,
it is a name he took-from-us!"
(This, I the Storyteller, was told by The-Old-Ones—
the ones still living.)

"To the Cherokee,
this name Indian,
means People-of-the-Creator.
This Creator,
the Cherokee call by many names.
But He is one:

"The-Mysterious-One;
The-Maker-of-All-Things;
The-One-Who-Gives-Life;
The-One-Who-Lives-Through-the-Clouds;
The-Great-Spirit;
The-Creator;
He is Ye-HO-Waah."
(This, I the Storyteller, was told by The-Old-Ones.)

Chapter Five

The-Ancient-Ones,
who came before The-Old-Ones,
also spoke of this Creator and told me:
"He is The-One-Who-Is-Three, but is One."

This is a great mystery!
But it is a mystery
    like the many forms the water from our rivers takes.
It is like water flowing down from high in the mountains;
it is like water in the cold moons that makes ice;
it is like the morning water that rises in a mist.
But it is the same river; it is the same water.
It is three; it is one.

These names,
The-Ancient-Ones spoke of The-One-Who-Is-Three:

"The-Elder-Fires-Above;
The-Ones-Who-Live-Through-the-Clouds;
The-Three-Beings-Above."
(This, I the Storyteller, was told by The-Ancient-Ones.)

To each of these three Elders-Of-Fire
    the Cherokee have given a name.
"Unethlanuhi [Oo-net-la-nuh-hee]—The-Great-One;
Atanvti [A-tanv-ti]—The-One-Who-Joins-With-Us;
Usqahula [Us-qu-hu-la]—The-Spirit-One."

Among themselves
—not among Those-Who-Are-Related-to-Nothing—
the Cherokee *are* spoken of
    as The-Real-People-of-the-Creator,
—the Cherokee Indian—
they have been here since the beginning of time.

(This, I the Storyteller, was told by The-Old-Ones.)

Crowdancing's mother grew up
    in what would one day be called Wolfetown,
of the Eastern Band of the Cherokee;
A place not far from the Cherokee Mother-Town
    of Kituwa,
the birthplace, the homeland,
the Mother-Town of the Cherokee people.

Kituwa was home to The-Real-People
    before they went-out into many villages.
It is a place deep within the sacred mountains
    of Carolina-North—the oldest mountains
    in what some will call the New-World . . .
but it is not new—it is very old.

Kituwa is a sacred land just beyond the Qualla Boundary;
an old Out-Town settlement of early days;
a place of magnificent running water,
the sound of majestic elk and howling wolves
    as night falls,
and mountains that awaken each day
    with the fullest hue of blue-green haze.

The earliest Cherokee people,
many life times before they were divided
    into the Eastern Band and the Western Band,
called these mountains Shaconage [sha-con-O-hey];
The-Land-of-Blue-Smoke;

Chapter Five

The-Mountains-of-Blue-Haze;
The-Smoky-Mountains.

It is a land where there is a forever-haze;
A haze created by the spirit essence of life
    as it is released from the mountain's grand kindred
    and family of plants and trees.
An essence that appears as a cool green vapor
    that mingles with the brilliant light of the blue sky.
Some say . . .
"It is the breath of the Little-People!"
And it smells of wild spearmint and berry-cider.

At the centre of this ancient village
—Kituwa—
once stood the sacred council house of seven sides
    lifted high above the village-flat,
where it sat atop a mound of earth—
a hill that grew to the height of seven men
    on The-Day-the-Earth-Shook-and-Roared.

Within this sacred house
    was held an ancient wooden ark
    and within this box of wood
    were kept the sacred symbols of the Cherokee
    from olden days,
hallowed items which no man was to see.

Just below the council house and sacred mound,
laid a village-square smoothed flat with human toll,
and covered thin with sand.
On this square were held the village rites—
the dances, the festivals, the ceremonies, the games.
Most every day, there within,
some ageless and mystic tradition took place.

Covered arbors stood *near* the village-square
    as rooms to outside-meet;
arbors made with tall poles of cane and wood,
and roofs of cane or thatch.

In summer days of balm and heat,
loved ones would gather to sleep and eat and tell their tales
    beneath these open arbors
    of wooden posts with roofs of cane
    in-which to shade themselves from summer's heat.

Throughout the village town,
within a hands-breath
    of the council house and square and arbors,
were spread many Houses-That-Are-Square—
houses made of wattle and daub.
Homes of one room, or two,
framed with logs from trees,
and woven with branches and river cane,
like the weaving of a basket.

These homes were covered in mud and grass
    and roofed with thatch and bark
    from plants and trees that were easy to find
    within the mountains of this vast forest land.
These were the homes
    in which each of the Cherokee
    lived and breathed and ate and played . . .
and in these homes,
some still live today.

In days of bitter cold and snowy moons,
the family would often flee The-House-That-Is-Square
    to The-House-That-Is-Hot—the *Asi* [Awe-see];
a small encumbered winter hut

Chapter Five

in the rounded form of a basket,
placed down-side-up.

This smaller home sat
    just outside The-House-That-Is-Square.
A lodge of plastered
    mud and hair and skin and grass and clay,
with but one opening that-is-small.
An opening to be entered as you bend headlong,
and in which you lay to chant or sing or pray or sleep,
each by the embittered heat of its winter's fire.

It was a place two great storytellers
    may freely barter their truth and lies
    as one spoke the common speech.

"Let us sit and tell our tales!"

And within these walls where-they-could-not-stand,
where it is always bitter-hot,
they talked and sweated and smoked.

When they had had enough,
they crawled from this sweltering lodge as they sang
    and walked the river's path,
where they plunged themselves seven times,
and called aloud Ye-HO-Waah's name.
The-Houses-That-Are-Square,
The-Houses-That-Are-Hot,
The-Arbors-of-Posts-and-Roofs-of-Cane,
were all encased by planted fields
    of corn and squash and beans and gourds;
each family,
an allotted plot to plant.

The corn was sown in smallesh-hills,
beans growing up each stalk,
and spreads of squash and gourds
    between the hills of corn.

And birdhouses made of hollow gourds
    hung throughout the gardens
    in-which lived the saw-winged-swallows and martins,
who chased away the lingering crows,
who came to feed upon the Indians' plants each day.

As far back as there is uttered Cherokee tales-to-tell,
Crowdancing's mother's family
    were spirit-guides and healers,
teachers, priests, and medicine men.
And those who grow food and care for the land
    of the Cherokee Indian.

But once the Cherokee were forced west
—on The-Trail-Where-They-Cried—
Crowdancing's mother's people stayed behind
    and hid-out in The-Mountains-of-Blue-Haze.
And there—it is said—
Crowdancing's family can still be found today.

Most speak of the ancestors and descendants
    of Crowdancing's mother
—those who came before and those who came after—
as Cartiers, or Carters,
because they once made wagons and carts
    for the Cherokee people.
Wagons and carts that were drawn by hand
    or pulled by horses or small white dogs,
dogs who did not bark,

Chapter Five

found in most every Cherokee village
    in ages of days gone by.

There is little written down
    about these wagons and carts and horses and dogs,
before Kuh-Luhm-Buhs and De-Soto are said to have
    brought them to this primal land.
But among The-Old-Ones there are spoken tales;
and from The-Ancient-Ones there are drawings in caves,
on animal skins,
and on stones that grow from the ground.
And there are beads and crystals and feathers that talk.

All speak of an ancient world
    when all of these things were so.

*"Do not be deceived by what others have said,
when these things they did not see.
For the Cherokee only show what he wishes to-be-seen.
We have always had wagons and carts and horses
    and dogs to pull them . . . why would we not?
But these things we did not let the outside world see,
because the outside world we did not trust.
From their eyes we hid these things in our caves
    and in our places of hiding, high in our mountains.*

*"When these outsiders were gone away,
we brought these hidden things back into our villages
    and there we used them every day.
This is the way it has always been, this is the way it will be!"*
(This, I the Storyteller, was told by The-Ancient-Ones.)

There was even a time
    when the Cherokee haughtily displayed the bones
    of these ancient horses and circular pieces of stone

that represented their ancient carts,
each placed about their necks,
sewn into their belted otter-skin and deer-skin robes,
their turkey feathered cloaks,
and wrapped around their upper arms and wrists.

You could hear the rattle of these adornments
    as the men walked,
especially those of the Long-Hair Clan,
who would vainly strut and twist as they paced
    from one end of the village to the other for all to admire;
their long-dark-hair flowing in all directions
    as it was blown by the wind.
And in the sacred mountains
    and valleys of the Eastern Band of the Cherokee,
just off in the distance,
you can still hear the soft jangle of these rattles today.

There are others
—Those-Who-Are-Related-to-Nothing—
who believe Crowdancing's mother's descendants
    to be the Little-People who inhabit the woods and fields
    and seldom make themselves known
    to their human inhabitants.
But like the Hill-Dwellers,
I know this notion is falsely formed,
simply because the Cartiers have long made their home
    among the Little-People of these mountains,
and not because the Cartiers are Little-People themselves.
For the Cartiers are of an energy source of a different kind
    than the Little-People.
It is a forever form.
Like the Hill-Dwellers,
their ancient ones have become The-Immortal-Ones.
Their energy . . . is of-the-soul.
Once you make the acquaintance of the Cartiers

Chapter Five

—whether by sight or sound or movement or emotions
    felt within—
you will know,
from then forward,
when you are in their midst.
For something stirs deep within each soul,
when you enter into their sacred-space.

With such a grand and illustrious shared tradition
    of these two families,
it is somehow not known,
or perhaps not yet known,
how this man from the very heart of Ireland,
and this woman
    from the sacred Cherokee mountains of Carolina-North
    met and married,
but this they did;
it is a truth that no-one disputes.
And into this noble linage of clans,
Crowdancing was born,
on the seventh day of December, 1657.

"O-E-A . . . Yah!
What I have said is true.
And I, the Storyteller, do tell this tale."

Chapter Six: Cherokee Naming Ceremony

*"What is in my name? Perhaps
nothing. Perhaps everything!"*

Summer 1659–The Storyteller:

It was said by his mother
    that *"Crowdancing danced with the crows,
    before he could walk."*
The first time his mother and father
    noticed Crowdancing's special bond with his namesake
—the crow—
was an early morning,
just like the one on which he was born;
except this time it was summer.
On this momentous morning,
Crowdancing was almost two years old,
and not yet walking.

It was barely sunrise
    when Crowdancing's parents awoke
    to the enthusiastic sound of dancing crows,
just outside their open window.
The sound was one his mother recalled
    with intense fondness;
it was as if a memory came to life
    just as it had occurred but two years before.
The young Crowdancing,
who slept on a mattress of cane
    covered in the skin of a mountain lion—the panther,
was not in his bed.
His parents quickly arose to follow the sound of the crows.

As they stepped outside
    into the Creator's Sacred-Place of grass and soil and air,
the birds of three took gentle flight.
And there,
in the middle of the crows' former dance ground,
was the young boy,
deep in a meditative dance, eyes closed,
with one long black crow feather,
which he held and shook in his left hand—
the hand closest to his heart.

Crowdancing was dancing and singing and praying
    an unknown chant,
but with syllable-sounds and a mystical rhythm,
just as real and lush as any ancient Celtic or Cherokee
    sacred hymn, or psalm, or story.

Crowdancing's words were flowing,
just as the words Ye-HO-Waah gave **me, the Storyteller,**
on the day Crowdancing was born;
and all the stories I pull from the Storyteller's Bag
—this Bundle-of-Talk—

Chapter Six

I will tell to you,
in their mystical form,
and with their sacred meaning.

A Cherokee child will have a name given to him
     within a few days of birth.
A name placed upon him by his parents;
a Cherokee priest;
or a Beloved Woman of the tribe.

Later in life,
the child will earn a new name,
as one-who-is-older.
A new name based on something
     that sets-him-apart from those around him.

But for Crowdancing,
at this special moment in time,
and even though he was still but a child,
his birth name was fixed upon him
     as his name-for-all-times.
And on this most uncommon day-in-history,
was the beginning of Crowdancing's
     most uncommon days-to-come—
a future no one yet foresaw,
but one so mystically and visually presented
     none-the-less.
For no clearer sign could have been offered
     to foretell one's destiny,
than this extraordinary Cherokee naming ceremony,
offered by a hover of enchanted crows,
and a young Indian boy,
as he delightfully sang and twirled and danced,
in the trance of his first *Dance-of-the-Enchanted-Crow*.

On this special day,
another gift was also given to Crowdancing.
He was given the gift of *forever-enchantment!*
The ability to experience the enchantment of his youth,
into all his days-to-come.

While the children around him
     would soon outgrow their youthful sense
     of wonderment and awe,
Crowdancing would forever
     let his spirit and soul come out and play;
And this gift would not simply *stay-with-him*
     as he grew in age;
the gift would *expand-and-grow*
     with each moon and every new sun;
as each moon and sun came
     and as every sun and moon went;
as the sun and moon
     joined in that magical moment each day,
with the touch of their spherical hands,
or a kiss of their shifting light.

"O-E-A . . . Yah!
What I have said is true.
And I, the Storyteller, do tell this tale."

Chapter Six

Chapter Seven: Days of Fun and Folly

*"We must let our spirit and soul come out to play,
or they will die.
For it is in this simple act of sacred play
we find our meaning and our path.
It is within
the sacred-space
of our expanded-imagination
that we find a peace and joy.
A peace and joy that far surpasses
all our humble ability
to understand."*

1660-1666—The Storyteller:

The story is told, **and I, the Storyteller, do tell this tale.**
A story of youthful days of fun and folly,
as spoken among the Cherokee,
and stories held deep within the Storyteller's Bag.

In many ways,
Crowdancing was just an ordinary young boy
    of the Long-Hair Clan of his mother;
a boy who filled his time
    making friends with the animals of the woods,
in the essence of nature;
a boy who learned skills from the village craftsmen,
the hunters, the warriors, the priests,
and the medicine people of his tribe;
a boy who hunted and fished,
with dart and spear,
with blowgun and trap,
with arrow and bow;
a boy who played Cherokee kickball and marbles,
stickball and chunkey—with the-great-stonewheel-and-stick.
All of these games taught him
    the ancient ways of life and warfare,
of hunting and work,
of alliance and love,
that all young boys of the Cherokee must learn.

Crowdancing was also a boy who loved-much,
and cared-with-greatness for his younger sister,
Derdriu [D-EHR-dra]—The-Pensive-One,
who came from another tribe
    and was embraced into the Long-Hair Clan
    when she was but six new moons in age.

Chapter Seven

He looked up to his older brother,
Airell [AIR-ell]–The-Noble-One,
named for the Irish blood of his father,
yet a member of his mother's clan,
like all Cherokee children.

He was a boy who loved his mother and father–
The-One-Who-Is-Born-at-Night and Seaspar;
a boy who respected his uncles, his aunts,
his grandmothers, his grandfathers–
the Hill-Dwellers and Cartiers,
of the Mountains-of-Blue-Haze.

Crowdancing was a boy who spent his days-of-youth
    within the Appalachian Valley
    and the Great Smoky Mountains
    of what would soon become a colony–Carolina.
A new colony,
to be set down in an old land and renamed
    for an English King–King Charles the First,
King Carolinus to some.
An honor bestowed upon the land of the Cherokee
    by this King's son–King Charles the Second.
An honor the land did not wish to receive,
but which it acquired . . . all-the-same.

Not far ahead in days-to-come,
this colony would be separated into two sisters.
The upper-land to be called Carolina-North,
and separated on the symbolic maps
    from her southern sister, Carolina-South;
maps created by non-Indian explorers,
who did not ask to make these marks,
or set these foreign names.

It was in these valleys
        and mountains and streams and woods,
that Crowdancing found enchantment
        each day of his youth.
Enchantment and adventures he delightfully shared
        with his friends.
The ones he chose . . . as Close-Ones.

"O-E-A . . . Yah!
What I have said is true.
And I, the Storyteller, do tell this tale."

Chapter Seven

Chapter Eight:
The Close-Ones
The-Fair-One

"Though we may have many we call friends,
there are but few we call Close-Ones,
and they are the ones that make all the difference!"

1667-1671—The Storyteller:

The House With Seven Sides

The-Fair-One, had sun-touched golden skin and raven hair
    held in two long braids of three strands each—
one braid to frame each side of her delicate face
    and dangling almost to her waist.
The-Fair-One was the oldest of Crowdancing's friends
    and knew the ways of the Cherokee well.

All the boys of the village had eyes for The-Fair-One,
yet she paid them no mind.

Though sacred pipes were mostly made by Cherokee men,
The-Fair-One, of the Red-Paint Clan,
Those-From-Whom-the-Healers-Come,
created many.

Her grandest pipe?
A ceremonial Pipe-of-Seven-Stems.
A pipe used by the Cherokee priests in sacred rites
     held but once each year.
Ceremonies held within the great council house,
of the Mother-Town of the Cherokee.

This sacred lodge,
like the Pipe-of-Seven-Stems,
had seven-sides,
with a special place for each member
     of the seven clans to sit,
as they would smoke the sacred pipe,
as the chief
—The-Red-Chief-of-War or The-White-Chief-of-Peace—
would talk his speech;
or as a priest might sing his hymn;
or as a messenger might share his news
     from outside the Mother-Town.
Every village had its sacred council house with seven sides,
though Those-Who-Are-Related-to-Nothing,
would sometimes speak of them as round.
In this, their eyes deceived.

The men, the women, the children
     all came to this house for many sacred gatherings,

Chapter Eight

for ceremonies, for festivals, for talks of peace—
each taking his rightful place within its walls.

And the men,
and sometimes a Woman-of-War,
came . . . when there was a war to plan.

The Blue Clan,
the Bird,
the Deer,
the Long-Hair,
the Red-Paint,
the Wild-Potato,
and the Wolf Clan—
they all came to meet at this lodge,
many times between each new moon.

The Red-War-Chief,
the White-Peace-Chief,
the Cherokee-Priests,
the Medicine-Men,
the Counselors,
and the common people of the tribe—
they all came to this council house when they were called.
And at the centre of this great house,
the eternal flame forever burned.
A Fire-Priest always present to keep it lit.

Since Near-the-Time-of-Creation,
until The-Time-That-Is-Now,
I have seen the smoke from this flame
    always afloat.
And the fire . . . it still burns today.

If you had traveled past the olden mound
    of the Mother-Town in Days-of-Past;
if you travel there in Days-of-Now;
or if you travel there in Days-to-Come;
you will see the smoke
    lifting gently toward the clouds
    from deep within the womb of her mother.
That was then,
this is now,
and it will always be.

Within the Storyteller's Bag is a bundle of ash
    taken from this eternal flame,
to forever tell the story of The-House-With-Seven-Sides.

"O-E-A . . . Yah!
What I have said is true.
And I, the Storyteller, do tell this tale."

The Pipe With Seven Stems

The bowl of The-Fair-One's seven-stem pipe
    was formed from a soft white stone;
a stone she selected and cut from an old quarry
    just a few day's journey
    to the North and West of her village.
This place would one day be called Knox-Ville;
so named for a man called Henry Knox;

This man,
The War-Chief of the Great-Father
    of the new white nation,
the one called Washington,
was taking away the Cherokee's land;

Chapter Eight

stealing it,
and giving it to whom he chose.

The Cherokee people held many talks
    with these two men in great labor toward peace,
talks that were good,
but this peace . . . it did not come.

Crowdancing often traveled with The-Fair-One
    on her quests for these pipe stones.
The-Fair-One once told him,
"These stones are sacred;
they have life;
they breathe the same air as you and me;
they were placed here by the Creator
    to make our sacred pipes;
and this is the task the Great-One has given to me."
On their return from the sacred stone quarry
    one summer's day,
The-Fair-One and Crowdancing took an old Indian trail
    near The-Mountain-Where-It-Thunders.

On the day I first told this tale,
this trail was the lowest pass
    through the great Thunder-Mountain,
though a new trail
—a New-Found-Trail [Newfound Gap]—
would one day soon be found
    as an even lower and easier path.
But of this new way,
The-Fair-One and Crowdancing did not yet know.

On their way through the old Thunder-Mountain trail,
darkness began to lower its shade,
when the two travelers came upon a great

and mystical place.
At this place,
they chose to spend the night.

"O-E-A . . . Yah!
What I have said is true.
And I, the Storyteller, do tell this tale."

The Enchanted Lake

As the sun began to sit behind the mountain
    and a full moon began to rise above its crest,
Crowdancing and The-Fair-One
    found a small alcove of a cave
    just within the side of a cliff looking down over
    a small and parched valley of sandy-loam soil below.

There were animal tracks of many kinds
    leading downward from the bluffs to the dry earth;
but as they followed these tracks to the bottom of the trail,
the tracks no longer appeared.
As they walked back up to the cave,
they knew this was the place they would rest for the night.
It was a place where great visions were sure to be born.

With no food remaining in their bags,
for they had eaten the last portions of bread at the quarry
    to make room for the sacred stones,
they resolved to fast
    until they once again returned to their village.

After building a small fire,
fueled with the limbs and branches of fallen trees,
they shaped out small indentions in the soil

Chapter Eight

    in which to lay their hips;
and they gathered bunches
    of still-living branches of balsam fir,
as pillows placed beneath their heads.
And they slept.

That night,
both Crowdancing and The-Fair-One,
dreamed of great flocks
    of birds and animals and mysterious beings,
all gathering together at an enchanted lake
    where they came to drink and heal their wounds
    and make-well their sickness.

The next morning,
just as the first tinge of blue-green haze and light
    touched their eyes,
both Crowdancing and The-Fair-One
    were awakened by the sound
    of great flocks of geese and ducks
    and all manner of birds flying overhead,
then moving downward into the valley below.

At first they thought they were still dreaming;
but as they looked upon the last night's plot of sandy soil,
there before their eyes
    was an expanse of lavender-colored water,
an enchanted lake filled with water flowing red
    from springs to the west
    and blue from springs to the north,
with their brilliant colours blending together
    where the two springs met.

Within this most magnificent purple lake
        were fish of countless shapes
        and the largest turtles ever seen.

Deer of black and white and brown
        stood at the water's edge,
as did thick-furred-bears of the same colours.

Foxes, rabbits, animals big and small,
and of all types,
patiently drank and played—
each paying the others no mind.

And birds of all forms,
flocked as one,
above the watery depth.

The children had heard of this magical place
        by the village storytellers.
But this . . . this was much more than a faerie tale.
For they had found the great Medicine-Lake
        that stands within The-Space-That-Flows-Between—
a place long kept hidden,
to all but The-Enchanted-Ones.

Crowdancing and The-Fair-One sat
        and watched for what seemed but a short bit of time,
but in truth,
they sat in this place for the whole of the day.

As they finally breathed a different breath
        and stood and began
        their slow descent to the lake below,
the waters, the geese, the bears, the turtles

Chapter Eight

—ALL—
faded into the air like a morning's mist.

As the young ones completed their walk down the cliff
    to the spot of the mystical lake,
there they once again encountered
    only the sandy loam of the previous night—
but not one sign of water or spring.
And once again,
just as the night before,
there were animal tracks of all breeds of beast and foul,
each taking one last step . . . into nothing.

As Crowdancing and The-Fair-One
    resumed their journey home,
I, the Storyteller,
walked to the edge of the now-invisible-lake
    and picked up the feather of a wild turkey
    sticking upward from the soil,
the pointed tip being ever so moist.
I placed the feather in my Bag-of-Talk
    and took my leave.

"O-E-A . . . Yah!
What I have said is true.
And I, the Storyteller, do tell this tale."

The Remaking of Tobacco

As well as the Pipe-of-Seven-Stems,
The-Fair-One also made sacred pipes
    for the countless ceremonies
    the Cherokee priests held most every day.

The bowls of these pipes were made
        of graystone and bluestone;
stone she found in the Mountains-of-Blue-Haze
        and to which she added her elaborate forms and shapes.

One piece of bluestone,
she was given by Crowdancing—
a gift from his father.

*"This magical blue stone was passed to me
        from my ancestors;
it is from my homeland—it is from Eireann.
Its mother-stone is a rock that still stands tall
        in the midlands of that land.
And one day, you, my son,
will return to touch this sacred stone,
and gather another piece from its form,
to be placed in the Storyteller's Bag."*
(This, the old Irishman told Crowdancing,
and this, Crowdancing told The-Fair-One
        when he gifted her the stone.)

When she completed the carving of each pipe's bowls,
The-Fair-One would attach them to long softwood stems,
often made from the wood of a sassafras tree,
and filled and smoked,
only with remade-tobacco.

*"The tobacco for your pipes must come
        from the old Indian tobacco that grows wild
        in our mountains.
This plant must be pulled up,
and the seeds must be replanted,
in a sacred-place,
and in a sacred way.*

Chapter Eight

"The soil into which it is planted must be remade
    by plucking the wood
    from a tree that had been struck by lightning;
the wood must then be burned and tilled into the soil
    before you plant the seed."
(This, Crowdancing and The-Fair-One were told
by the old ones.)

Though they were still young,
Crowdancing and The-Fair-One twice attended
    the harvest ritual for the remaking of tobacco.
A ceremony always held at sunrise
    and overseen by a Cherokee priest.

After each of these two harvests,
the young pair followed the priest to the river
—the Tuckasegee [Tuck-a-see-gee]—
—Turtle Place—
for their first remaking ceremony;
and to the sacred white waters
    of the Oconaluftee [O-con-a-luff-tee].
The By-the-River, river,
for the second.

What becomes the Oconaluftee
    flows down from the high peaks
    of the Great Smoky Mountains
    and forms into creeks and streams and branches
    that converge and create the sacred river
    below the mountain.
The Oconaluftee then drains into the Tuckasegee
    near the Cherokee Mother-Town,
where ancient stone weirs
—shaped in great downward patterns of Vs—
open upstream and closed downstream,
can still be seen today.

In these great weirs,
the Cherokee have always stood to
    collect fish of many kinds for food.

At each of these enchanted rivers,
the remade tobacco was blessed with a sacred prayer,
sung by the sacred priest,
and repeated for six more chants.

"This is the way we remake the tobacco.
It is the same way from the time of the ancients.
This is how it must be done."
(This the priest told Crowdancing and The-Fair-One,
and this they understood.)

"It is only through this ceremony,
the sacred power will be placed into the plant.
If the tobacco is smoked,
and it is not remade,
it will cause the one who smokes it forever-harm."

From the stems of these pipes,
The-Fair-One draped leather strips of fringe,
and animal hair, and feathers, and coloured beads
    made of bone and stained with the sap of plants.
And The-Fair-One,
unlike the other makers of pipes,
added a tuff of rabbit fur just about the portion of the stem
    nearest the bowl.
These tuffs of fur were her special mark.
And I, the Storyteller, have one of these sacred pipes
    held inside my Bundle-of-Talk.
Just inside the Storyteller's Bag.

Chapter Eight

The beads used for The-Fair-One's pipes were
     stained in the sacred colours of the Cherokee—
white for birth and peace;
red for youth and strength;
blue for trouble and old age;
and black for death and decay.

Each colour,
a symbol for each of the four directions:
White for the south—The-Place-of-Peace;
Red for the east—The-Sun-Land;
Blue for the north—The-Place-of-the-Cold-Wind,
and Black for the west—
The-Place-Where-It-Always-Grows-Dark.
Other Cherokee pipes would sometimes
     include three more tribal colours:
Yellow for the mysterious Land-Above-Where-We-Stand;
Brown for The-Land-Below-Where-We-Stand;
and Green for The-Place-Where-We-Stand.

On one memorable day,
a story now kept in the Storyteller's Bag,
the White Chief commissioned The-Fair-One to
     make three special pipes
     to be used to honor the mysterious
     One-Who-Is-Three—
     Who-Lives-Through-the-Clouds.

From one pipe,
The-Fair-One draped an eagle feather;
from another,
The-Fair-One draped the feather from a red bird;
and from the third hung the feather of a mourning dove.

These feathers she was given
      by the One-Who-Collects-the-Sacred-Feathers—Songbird.
These three pipes were only used once,
in a ceremony no man outside the Cherokee people
      has ever known;
it is a story that has been lost.
And I, the Storyteller,
am the first to tell this tale.
I hold deep within the Storyteller's Bag,
the feathers from these sacred pipes.

The ancient Pipe-Keepers then spoke these words,
      "Some call our sacred pipes, peace pipes.
This is a lie; it is not true!
The sacred pipes of the Cherokee—
those made by the Men-Who-Make-Pipes
      and by The-Fair-One—
we do not call by this name.
These sacred pipes
      are not smoked without sacred meaning
      and honored tradition;
they are not smoked with those we do not trust;
and these pipes are not taken into one's hand
      without permission of a Cherokee priest;
for they are sacred instruments
      used only for sacred ceremonies."

The ancient Pipe-Keepers also told me that
      the sacred pipes of the Cherokee are
      always kept in a secret place of hiding by
      one of the tribe's Pipe-Keepers:
and they are wrapped in a sacred cloth that is white.

"Yes, these pipes have been used for a call for peace,
this is much-truth," he said.
"But they are never called by-this-name."

Chapter Eight

The-Fair-One's three holy pipes were
        wrapped only in the fur of a white animal,
one without any blemish;
and The-Fair-One's father was the only one who
        knew the place of their keeping.
But, before this man passed,
he gave **me, the Storyteller,**
the pipe's feathers.
But, of the place of the pipes keeping,
no one any longer knows.

This he also told to me,
"Before the days of Crowdancing and The-Fair-One,
some of our Cherokee sacred pipes were long-like-the-river,
the stems reaching out as long as one's arm,
with heavy bowls of stone carved in the form
        of a buffalo, a bear, a deer, a turtle, an eagle.
Of how these pipes were once used,
the truth we do not know.
But of their life,
it is a most-certain-truth."

The-Fair-One's father also told me
        that the sacred pipes of the Cherokee all have meaning.
This he said,
"All-That-Is—this is the meaning of our sacred pipes.
The bowl *of the pipe is a symbol of the world . . .*
it is where we live;
the stem *. . .*
it is our link to this world,
the Sacred-Space that connects all things;
the tobacco *. . .*
it is all that has life,
all that is created by the Great Spirit;
the smoke *that lifts up from the pipe . . .*
it is our prayers, and the prayers of all that is created,

(This is what I, the Storyteller, have been told,
and this is what I know.)

"O-E-A . . . Yah!
What I have said is true.
And I, the Storyteller, do tell this tale."

Chapter Eight

Chapter Nine:
The Close-Ones
Kween

*"From whence we came
is not nearly as important as where we are now,
and where we are going."*

1667-1671—The Storyteller:

The Beloved Women

Kween, of infinite red hair and the lightest skin,
was *from another place.*
The place, perhaps,
of Crowdancing's father's homeland—
the place of blue-green water and emerald-green grass.
Or from the land of Angles—England.

This it is thought because,
unlike the Cherokee,
she was named for an English queen,
but had lived among the Cherokee
        since before she was born.
Some of the Beloved Women say,
"Kween is more Cherokee than the Cherokee themselves."

As a youth, Kween loved to create beautiful things
        and was often found sitting beneath a canopy
        of sycamore, maple, and hemlock trees
        at the edge of the Oconaluftee River,
singing a sacred song,
and sewing the most lovely turkey feathered cloaks,
and other Cherokee clothing and blankets
        made from the bark of trees, animal skin, strands of hemp,
and animal hair woven together
        in special symbols and shapes
        like that of a patchwork quilt.

As a member of the Blue Clan—
The Panthers,
the Wild Cats,
The-Ones-Who-Use-the-Blue-Plant—
Kween knew well the way of the blue-medicine
        and brought healing and protection to the village children—
though she was still very young in age herself.
And if a woman were to have a baby,
young Kween was often there with the mother-to-be
        and the midwife to assist in any way needed.

"Jump down young one,
take your watered bed and flee,
the ugly one is coming for you."
This she would sing until the little one was born.

Chapter Nine

As One-Who-Helps-Them-Jump-Down,
Kween was sometimes honored
    by giving a child his first name.
The mother and midwife and Kween
    would then take the new baby to water,
where he was immersed seven times.

If the water was frozen over or laden with snow,
the child was rolled seven turns in the snow
    as if this white covering for the ground
    was his first baby blanket.

The child would then be bathed
    with a mixture of liquid made from the blue plant
    taken from Kween's medicine pouch and ably applied
    to protect the little one from sickness.
This sacred bath would be repeated each new moon
    of the child's first year of life.

If it was a girl who was born,
the village would soon hear a young Wren
    singing a happy song,
for she knew this new one
    would soon beat-the-grain for bread,
and leave lost seeds behind on which to feed.

But, if it was a boy who was born,
the Wren would sing a sad song,
for he knew the young one would soon come hunting
    with his blowgun or bow.

"O-E-A . . . Yah!
What I have said is true.
And I, the Storyteller, do tell this tale."

A Woman of Mystery

One memorable summer day,
just before the first time when the-leaves-begin-to-fall,
Crowdancing and Kween were out hunting
    for the medicine plant Kween used
    when helping children jump-down.
They had left the Mother-Town
    just as the sun rose above The-Mountains-of-Blue-Mist
    and had walked south till the sun was high in the sky,
their packs now full of the blue plants and its roots;
it was time to go home.

With their characteristically curious natures,
Crowdancing and Kween
    decided to travel back to the village by a different path,
by way of a clear-water stream
    they had encountered on their morning's journey.

As the sun lowered itself toward the mountains,
they came upon a swampy area of land
    where the flowing stream disappeared into a bog
    where the water collected and stood low;
the moist earth full of ancient stumps and stones
    and the most unusual types of plants
    the children had ever seen.

It was at this place that Crowdancing and Kween
    met a-woman-of-mystery
    they had never before encountered.
The woman was very old;
this they saw by her long white hair
    that looked of the coming winter snows.
But as they came closer,
the woman did not seem old at all.
She had the most beautiful copper skin

Chapter Nine

with no creases and folds
    like the older women of their village,
and her breasts were exposed and smooth
    like that of a young girl,
for she was wrapped only from her waist to her knees
    in the softened-skin of a white-tailed deer.

Even in the summer,
the girls and women in the Mother-Town
(except for those-who-toddle-about)
covered their breasts,
wearing thin dresses of animal skins and feathers and bark
    they wrap from shoulders to knees,
pinned between the breasts with pieces of sharpened bone,
and belted at the waist with wide strips of animal cloth.

But this woman . . .
she was only wrapped at the waist.
And she was digging . . .
prodding the earth for something near the edge of the water,
a carrying-basket made of split-cane at her side,
the kind of basket you fill and tie to your back
    when you walk.
As she saw the children approaching,
the woman lifted her eyes,
then stood.
But she did not seem alarmed.
The woman stood tall and erect and slender,
her legs well-shaped,
her entire proportions pleasing to the eyes.
She was the most elegant woman Crowdancing
    had ever seen.

It was Kween who asked the first questions,
"What is it you do. Who are your people?"

"I am of the ancient ones of the Blind-Savannah Clan
of the Cherokee—the Bear Clan, the Raccoon Clan,"
the woman spoke.

"We do not know this clan," Crowdancing replied.

"Ha! You speak the truth and your words are sad.
You now call us the Wild-Potato Clan
—The-Ones-Who-Gather-Wild-Roots—
for the people of my clan
have always gathered wild potatoes for food
and boiled them to eat,
or beaten them into flour for our bread—of this you know.
But we are also gatherers of many kinds of roots
and tubes and plants that hide themselves from sight.
We gather these plants from below the ground
where they are full of power and strength
and medicine from Ye-HO-Waah."
This sacred speech the woman spoke.

"How do you know where to find these plants?"
questioned Kween,
for she had been taught of many plants-which-do-not-hide,
but of these abundant plants-that-are-blind,
she did not know.

"We have been shown by our ancestors
where these plants-with-roots-for-food
and tubes-for-food hide.
And our ancestors were taught this by Ye-HO-Waah.
We have always cared for this mystic land
that hides below the ground.
But of our old-clan-name,
the Blind-Savannah,
ye young ones do not know.

Chapter Nine

And I am the last of the rambles of the Blind-Savannah,
so you will not know of where they hide, if I do not tell,"
and this she did.

Crowdancing and Kween helped the woman gather
    the wild plants until her basket
    was overflowing with many roots and tubes and plants
    of four different shapes and forms.
And on this day,
Crowdancing and Kween
    learned many things they did not know,
from this woman of an ancient clan.
The woman told them about
    the beginning of *Savannah* [sa-van-NAH] of the old days;
of the Blind-Savannah, the Bear, the Raccoon—
the clans from which her people first came.

"To-flourish-unspoiled,
this is Savannah;
others say the food within the soil is Raana (ray-ah-NAH)—
beautiful, unspoiled.
These names . . . they are the same."
These words the woman said.

"The food we take from the earth
    can live there blind within the soil
    to-flourish-unspoiled-in-beauty forever—
and taken only when needed.
This untouched food,
as it hides from our eyes,
in the womb of our mother,
can be pulled-up above the soil
    and feed the Cherokee in the-days-that-are-hot
    and the-days-that-are-cold;
in the-days-the-leaves-fall and the-days-of-planting."
These words the woman spoke.

"These plants inside the dismal mud
  in the land that is low and near the river,
we pull-up and store.
We cut them into pieces and place them in the sun to dry.
They are blind within the womb,
but then they see.
When we eat them,
we place them again into the water
  and they are made new,
as before they were born."
These words the woman said.

"This food from the hallowed ground,
we pull-up and store in our caves,
in our storehouses of wood and clay,
in our baskets buried beneath the soil,
close by where we live;
in this way,
we keep them near and hunger far."
These words the woman spoke.

"The Blind-Savannah
  have always foraged for these plants
  that hide inside the earth;
a place from which they cannot see us,
and we cannot see them.
But we . . . know where they hide—
this the Great Spirit has taught us,
and this you now know."

The woman told them about the ancient ones
  who would rise early and go to gather these roots
  before the sun was high in the sky,
or at the edge of night,
before the moon had risen.

Chapter Nine

"It is best to gather these plants beneath the soil
*   when the air is cold," she said.*

"And this Place-Where-We-Stand is a great bowl,
a dish,
a cup in-where the water flows and stands
*   as marsh and swamp, as bog and basin.*
Some of this water you see today
*   will flow out into a great river below us*
*   that will one day take our name—the Savannah;*
I do not lie, I tell the truth . . . O-E-A!"
These words she said.

The woman also told to them an ancient story
    of the Bear and the Raccoon—
other names for which her clan at one time was known.
She told them they must soon leave this place
—before the moon was high—
and go home,
or what had happened to her people,
may happen to them as well.
And this is her tale.

"O-E-A . . . Yah!
What I have said is true.
And I, the Storyteller, do tell this tale."

The Lost Clan of the Blind Savannah

A long time ago,
there was a young boy and girl
    of the Blind-Savannah Clan of the Cherokee
    who went into the woods each day
    to pull-up the wild plants that hide beneath the soil.

But there in the woods, each day,
they saw that the bear and the raccoon
        had come before them and pulled-up all the roots.
This happened for many days,
so one day the children rose before the sun
        and went into the woods early.

On this day they found the bear and the raccoon
        as they were just beginning to pull-up the plants,
many plants of many forms and shapes.

The young girl spoke first
        and asked the bear and the raccoon,
"What is it you do? Who are your people?"

The bear and raccoon told them,
*"We are of the Bear and Raccoon Clans
—Those-Who-Gather-Beneath-the-Earth—"*
They each spoke of many things
        and the bear and the raccoon
        shared the food they had foraged with the children.

The bear, the raccoon, and the children
        soon became friends.
And they all met each morning at the break of day,
or just before the moon began to rise each night,
at the great swamp in the woods.
And each day the children stayed longer and longer,
until the moon was high in the sky,
or disappeared,
and the sun began to flash its first rays of light.

One day the bear and the raccoon
        took the children to the other side of the swamp
        and into the hidden mountain—

Chapter Nine

a place they could not see
     from where they stooped to pull the plants.
And here at this place was a magical village
     of bear-people and raccoon-people,
and they danced, and they ate, and they played games,
from morning until night.
The children soon began to take part
     in the great ceremonies and the food and the dance,
and this they did for many days.

There was no record of time in their minds
     and they let their spirits, even their souls,
come out to play.
For this special place was beyond both time and days.

When the boy and girl finally returned to their home,
their parents asked them where they had been.

"We were worried you had died," their mother said,
with great tears of joy in her eyes—
for her children who were lost for a year,
had now come home.

At first the children lied,
but this they could not do for long,
so they told their parents the truth.

"We have been with the bear and the raccoon
     at their home in the woods.
It is an enchanted place of mystery
     where we can eat and dance and play all day.
And only select-ones go out each day for food,
which they share with all.
The others stay behind in this magical place
     and do what they wish.

The children continued their story,
"The bear and the raccoon
*   and the bear-people and raccoon-people*
*   have asked us to come and live with them . . .*
and we have told them yes!
But they have also spoken and said
*   that any of our clan may come with us as well,*
for we are of the Blind-Savannah Clan—
a great sister to the bear and raccoon.
They wish all our family, and all our clan
*   to join us and live with the bear and the raccoon.*
There is food and dance and play for all."

The next day the children and their parents
    met with all the members of the Blind-Savannah Clan
    in the great council house.
They told them all of the kind invitation
    by the great bear and the raccoon
    who live in the magic land
    of the hidden mountain beyond the swamp.

All that heard their speech on that day
    knew that at times there was not enough food
    for the Cherokee people
    and that all must go out every day and search long
    and hard for the food to keep their life.

Chapter Nine

They also knew that at times
    there was great sadness and pain in the village,
and there was very little dance and play
    between the new moons
    that flow in and out like the river.

"What the bear and the raccoon offer us is good,"
the people thought.

After much debate,
most of the clan said, *"Yes, let us all go."*
Only a few said no.
They would stay behind.

On the next day,
the children and their parents and all but a few
    of the clan packed what they had on their backs,
into their carts,
on their horses,
and went into the woods to the great swamp
    and hidden village
    where the bear and raccoon people lived.

Those who went,
took with them the name Blind-Savannah
    and some even adopted the name Bear or Raccoon.
Those who stayed behind,
took the name Wild-Potato Clan—
for they were no longer one with the Savannah.
The Blind-Savannah were now gone!

Those who went into the woods that day
    were never seen again,
except at special times when the air-is-thin
    and The-Space-That-Flows-Between

overflows into the land of man.
On these special days,
and in special places,
one may still see an ancient one,
"just as you see me today."
(This the woman of mystery told the children.)

"For I am from this ancient clan,
the Blind-Savannah,
The-Immortal-Ones."
This the woman had spoke.

As Crowdancing and Kween listened to her final words,
they looked back to ask a question of their host
    who walked behind them sharing her tale,
but she was no longer there.
And the creek was once more flowing,
no sign of bog, or swamp;
no bowl where water stands!

As the children rushed home to tell their parents
    all they had learned,
I, the Storyteller,
went down to the place of the hidden swamp
    and I pulled up
    one of the plants-with-roots-beneath-the-earth,
and placed it in my Storyteller's Bag.
Within this bag,
the plant can still be found today.
And within the soul of this plant,
the story of the Blind-Savannah is forever held safe,
and can only be shared
    by the one who holds the Storyteller's Bag.

Chapter Nine

"O-E-A . . . Yah!
What I have said is true.
And I, the Storyteller, do tell this tale."

Chapter Ten:
The Close-Ones
Eoin

"Knowledge is more than knowing;
it is feeling and sensing and hearing and touching.
True knowledge embraces all the senses,
in their highest dimension,
coming together as one.
It is only then,
that we know the choice we must make."

The Young Warrior From Four Lands

Eoin, (Ee-nn) was the only one in the village
    with twisted hair;
hair that was as black as the Cherokee,
yet curled about in rings-that-hang.
Like Kween,
Eoin came from another land.
Some called him oh-MAHN,
an ancient Hebrew name;
these say that he is a descendent of Job,
a great man of God.
Some say he is from England.
Others say he is from Ireland or Scotland,
of great Celtic heritage.
All say he is Cherokee.

One morning, just as the sun began to rise,
the elders gathered at the river
    with the sacred Cherokee crystal
    and the sacred black and white beads
    in quest of Eoin's birthright.
That night these same elders called a special meeting
    of all the seven clans into the village council house
    and these words they spoke.
"We have asked the crystal and the beads,
* and this is what they have told us.*
Eoin is of the Hebrew,
Eoin is of the lands called England and those of the Celts,
and Eoin is of the Cherokee.
Eoin is of all four places and four is our holy number.
We do not know how he is of four births,
but we know this is true."

Chapter Ten

The elders presented Eoin with a beaded belt
        of purple and white shell-beads in four patterns,
each pattern for one of his four births.
And into this belt,
they also placed the black and white beads
        the elders used in their quest of Eoin's birthright.

*"This talking belt will carry the story of Eoin's four births
        from days behind, to days ahead.
It must be kept in a hidden place of care
        so his story can be told."*

With these words spoken by the old ones,
Eoin handed the belt to **me, the Storyteller,**
and I placed it for keeping into my Storyteller's Bag.
And I, the Storyteller, do tell this tale.

Eoin was of the Wolf Clan
—Those-From-Whom-the-Red-Chiefs-Come—
and known for his sacred songs and chants;
for his skills as a warrior and protector in times of war;
and for his great skill in The-Little-Brother-of-War—
Cherokee stickball.
Eoin was the strongest
        of all the young boys in battle and in ball.

The Elders once said,
*"Eoin battles in the old way;
he always honors the traditions
        that have been passed down since before time.
Eoin will be a great man.
He will protect our tribe in days near,
and days far."*

The Tale of the Dragon

Eoin's greatest challenge,
in the days of fun and folly,
came one day when there was a call
    for young warriors and young medicine men
—one of each, from each clan—
to join together and hunt down and kill
    the great Uktena [ook-tay-nah].

All the Cherokee people
    knew of the Uktena—
The-Keen-Eyed-Horned-Serpent.
He was The-Evil-One-Who-Dwells-in-the-Land-Below
—a place where many great forces of foul-beings live,
and are sometimes drawn outward to the surface—
into the-middle-land,
for reasons we do not know.

On the morning of this memorable day,
a young Cherokee messenger had come rushing
    into the Kituwa village just at the time
      the sun strikes the council house
      from above the mountain.
The runner was shouting that a great beast
      had entered one of the two Cherokee villages
      to the west of Kituwa.
The villages that sit on the Tanasi River [Tennessee].
He told those who had gathered
    that most of his village had been awakened
    just before the sun rose up on the day before,

Chapter Ten

by piercing ghostly howls
    and a blinding light as great as the sun,
but the light was shining
    and moving about upon the land,
not downward from the sky.

Most of the villagers had escaped to their place of hiding,
but two warriors who stayed to fight the great beast
    had not returned.
The village messenger had been running all night,
sent to Kituwa to ask for their help
    in finding and killing the mystical serpent.

The elders of Kituwa
    were all called to gather at the council house—
the chiefs, the priests, the medicine men,
and the war-woman.
And the young messenger retold his tale to all.
As he spoke of the beast and described what he had seen,
they knew it to be the Uktena.
They told the messenger that he was blessed
    to have seen the beast and escaped with his life.

This Uktena is a mighty dragon,
larger in breadth than three of the biggest men
    of any village are wide,
and as long as six men are tall.
All along his thick snakelike body
    are white circles and shapes
    and impenetrable layers of silver-black scales
    that catch and throw-back any light
    from the sun or moon that touch its surface.
At a mid-place on each of his sides,
he can roll back his scales
    and spread out his hidden wings
    allowing him to fly in the sky as a bird.

But he can also fastly-dart along the ground
    as a massive snake that rattles the earth as he moves.
Though the creature has no legs,
he can stand tall and mighty upon his tail,
reaching as high as an ancient oak,
then drop his weight with such force
    that he can take down a tree,
a House-That-Is-Square,
or anything else that lies in his path,
creating a thunderous sound
    as that of an earthquake.

On the monster's head
    stands a pair of long stag horns with many points,
like the giant elk of the Cherokee forest.
And impressed deep into his forehead
    is a crystal-stone-jewel
    with a teardrop of red blood layered at its centre.
The crystal holds within its magical power
    the ability to control the minds
    of those who look upon its brilliant gleaming light.
And it gives anyone who holds it in his hands,
the ability to see into the future,
and control what happens.

It is said that anyone who peers into the dragon's eyes
    or looks upon the great stone above their gleam,
will run straight toward the dragon
    with the thought that he is running away.
And as he enters the dragon's space,
the beast wraps himself
    around the man or woman from foot to head,
slowly applying pressure until his captive . . .
becomes-no-more.
No one who has ever hunted the dragon,

Chapter Ten

or been drawn into his eyes,
has returned.

The elders asked the messenger
    in which direction the Keen-Eyed-Horned-Serpent
    had gone.

"He has gone upward
    toward the high point in the mountains."

This is when the elders
    selected chosen ones from each clan,
and put upon them the charge to hunt,
and kill,
the serpent.
And to bring back the diamonded-jewel
    it held above the space between his eyes.

From the Wolf Clan the elders selected Eoin
    and paired him with Crowdancing of the Long-Hairs.
Crowdancing was training
    in the ways of medicine and the priesthood;
Eoin, in the ways of war.

The elders did other pairings of different clans
    until two of each clans stood before them—
one of war,
and one of the medicine way,
in each group of two.

Eoin and Crowdancing were the youngest
    of all those selected,
but the elders knew their strength and vision
    were much greater than their number of days.

Eoin and Crowdancing spent that night in the Asi
    outside Eoin's House-That-Is-Square.
Eoin chanting his war chants,
scratching his arms, his back, his chest,
with a scratcher made of a single fang,
taken from a rattlesnake,
and tightly attached to a long stick
    with a prayer tie, made by Crowdancing,
hanging from its shaft
    and fashened to the quill of a single crow feather,
all held tightly in place with deer sinew
    painted a deep and crimson red.

The crow feather
    would connect Eoin's spirit with Crowdancing's
    as they undertook their journey together—
making their strength and vision as one;
the rattlesnake scratcher
    would give Eoin physical power and keenness
    as great as that of the mighty rattlesnake;
the prayer tie was used in prayer to the Creator
    in request for their ultimate success;
and the red deer sinew
—used as thread—
would give them the swiftness of a deer.
The pair would leave the fanged-scratcher and prayer tie
    within the Asi,
so their prayers would continue as they traveled.

Crowdancing spent the night having many visions
    and offering his prayers
    for their journey and their success—
singing and chanting
    the ancient prayer formulas
    he had been taught by the great medicine man—
He-Who-Knows-Most.

Chapter Ten

The next morning
      Eoin and Crowdancing both crawled out of the Asi
      at the rising of the sun and went to water.
Removing the breechcloths that covered their nakedness
      they plunged seven times beneath the surface.
As they came out of the water
      they replaced the cloth between their legs
      and added leather leggings,
leggings that came high
      up to the mid-point of their thighs.
They then added thick leather moccasins to their feet,
and deer skin shirts pulled down over their heads
      and reaching to their waists.
Unlike most of the warriors,
Eoin wore his hair long,
with raven curls hanging down against his shoulders.

Most Cherokee warriors wore their hair as a simple lock
      or knot atop their heads and adorned with feathers,
with much of the sides of their hair shaved or plucked
      just above the ears.
In this way they stood out in battle from other tribes,
as Cherokee warriors.

Crowdancing also wore his hair long,
as many of the Cherokee priests and medicine men did—
as a vow of strength.
But, from Crowdancing's Irish father's heritage,
his locks had a twist at the point where the bones
      come as a V below the front of his neck,
each twist pointing toward his heart.

During the night in which they slept,
both Eoin and Crowdancing had visions
      of a place where mulberries grow wild and tall;
a place where the bear and fox come to feast

on these berries-that-are-red.
And in these dreams
    they both saw a great dragon pulling up the plants
    and eating entire trees and bushes
    as though they were single bits of fruit.
They knew it would be a hard journey
    to Mulberry Place.
It was the highest point
    in the great Mountains-of-Blue-Haze.
But it was there they would find the Uktena.
This they knew.
He would be at this place,
feasting on the berries,
and lying in wait to kill all the animals
    who came to join him in his feast.

All that Crowdancing and Eoin took with them
    for their journey,
were two long-bows,
with seven notched arrows each,
held in dark leather quivers tied across their backs;
and two sacred pouches,
one each,
attached to the belts about their waists.

Within Crowdancing's pouch
    was a small bag of remade tobacco,
which he had kept from the ceremony
    he had taken part in with The-Fair-One
    and the priest,
just a few moons before;
two medicine plants that held great healing magic
    in case the boys were harmed;
a sacred white cloth of animal skin;
and three beads—one white, one black, one red.
In Eoin's bag was a knife made of flint;

Chapter Ten

remade tobacco given to him by Crowdancing;
a sacred pipe made by The-Fair-One;
and four other secret war items he always kept with him,
each item holding its personal tale of a past victory.

On the second day of their journey,
the pair—young priest and warrior—
reached The-Place-of-the-Mulberries.
And here they heard the most remarkable sounds
    they had ever encountered.
Piercing howls,
the shaking of the earth,
and the hissing of what had to be
    the grandest of all snakes;
for it could be easily heard,
even over the gale of a strong wind
    that blew hard on this day.

Though they could not yet see the serpent,
they knew he was near.
And they knew they must approach him slowly
    so he would not see and hypnotize them
    with his powerful gaze.

Both priest and warrior took a handful of tobacco
    and placed it on the ground in front of them,
and Crowdancing prayed a sacred prayer formula
    meant to calm the great beast into a sleep.
With this done,
they slowly continued their journey . . .
until there the great one lay in quiet slumber before them.

The magnificent dragon was covered
    in thick and shiny gray-black scales
    just as they had been told,

with great white spots
      along the entire length of his massive body.
In each legend of the Uktena
      it was said that the dragon could only be killed
      by placing an arrow into his heart,
"which rests at the seventh spot from his head."

But this seemed all too easy.
Eoin notched an arrow into his bow
      and aiming at the seventh white spot
      from the beast's head,
let loose the shaft.
The arrow hit its mark with perfect aim . . .
but rather than killing the dragon,
it merely angered it.
The serpent arose high on his tale,
letting lose another great howl
      and slammed against the earth,
only a hands-breath
      between the place where Crowdancing and Eoin stood.

"What have we done wrong?" Eoin shouted!

The dragon then unfurled his great wings
      from beneath his shiny scales
      and lifted his body from the ground between them.
The force of his unfurling wings
      knocked both Crowdancing and Eoin to the ground.

As the dragon rose
      to beyond the height of the nearest tree,
they knew they must move quickly,
because the dragon
      was now firing great beams of blinding light
      from the crystal-stone-jewel above his eyes.

Chapter Ten

And they knew no man had ever resisted
    the Keen-Eyed-Horned-Serpent's wicked stare.

It was in this briefest moment in time
    that Crowdancing was drawn
    into The-Space-That-Flows-Between,
where he instantly recalled a riddle he had been told
    by the medicine man who had been training him for
    almost four years.
A riddle about seven spots being seven openings,
seven orifices, seven outlets.
Crowdancing instantly reentered
    The-Place-Where-They-Stood and shouted at Eoin
    to shoot the dragon again,
but this time to aim his arrow into the dragon's mouth.

Just as the dragon opened his huge mouth
    in another deafening howl,
he drew both Eoin and Crowdancing
    into his stabbing gaze,
and toward him they both began to run.
But with his first step,
Eoin let loose the arrow,
piercing it clearly into the dragon's mouth,
through the back of his head and out the other side,
disappearing into the hazy blue sky.
The dragon dropped at once to the ground,
the stone-quartz-crystal falling from his forehead
    directly into Crowdancing's left hand.

"How did you know?" asked Eoin.

"The seventh spot from the head
    is the seventh opening in the head—
two eyes, two ears, two nostrils, and the mouth—

the seventh spot."
(This answer Crowdancing gave to Eoin.)

As they talked about what to do
     with the diamond taken from the dragon's head
—for fear it may be drawn into the wrong hands—
the poisonous black-red blood of the snake
     began to spill from beneath each of his scales,
and as it gushed out upon the ground
     surrounding the great serpent,
he began to slide in the thick liquid,
toward the mountain's lip.

As this dense muck of toxic blood
     pulled the dragon to the edge of the cliff,
he tumbled over the rim
     and began to roll again and again and again,
until, at last,
he came to the bottom the mountain,
tearing down hundreds of trees
     and finally coming to rest
     at a place on the Tuckasegee River
     where The-Great-Lake-of-Fountains
     would one day rise up.

Everywhere the dragon's blood
     had touched the green growth of tree or plant,
it shriveled up and died.
These poisoned plants and trees,
you can still see today.

Crowdancing and Eoin
     spent half of the day climbing down the mountain
     to the place where the dragon lay dead.
When they arrived,

Chapter Ten

the serpent was covered with great birds of prey
    and bears and panthers and foxes,
all devouring his meaty flesh—
as he once had devoured theirs.

All his scales,
once his stronghold against beast and man,
had been ripped and pulled from his flesh
    as he passed over rough stones and tall trees,
tossing and tumbling over and over
    as he rolled down the mountain's edge,
leaving layers of scales all aside the mountain—
scales that took the form of grey earthy sandstone
    everywhere they fell.
And these scales can still be seen,
all along parts of this mountain's slope today.

The young warrior and priest
    took out the sacred pipe
    that Eoin held within his pouch,
and placed a pinch of remade tobacco into its bowl,
offering their prayers of smoke to Ye-HO-Waah
    for their success against the powerful dragon foe.

They both sat and smoked from the pipe
    and watched the birds and beasts
    devour the entire Keen-Eyed-Horned-Serpent,
until all that was left
    were his horns and his bones.

From that day forward,
if a man who stands atop Mulberry Place
    [Clingman's Dome],
and looks downward upon the lake below
    [Lake Fontana],

he can still see the poisonous effects of the great serpent
        upon all the trees and land
        he touched during his great fall.

And at the lake below
        can still be found pieces of the dragon's bones
        washing up at the water's edge on a sunny day.
And but a short journey from this place at the river's edge,
there is a trail that will one day take the serpent's name—
the Tail-of-the-Dragon.

I then asked both Eoin and Crowdancing
        if I may take the dragon's-stone-crystal
        and keep it in a place of safety inside my
        Bundle-of-Talk.
They both agreed.
This was the only place
        where the mystery of the powerful stone
        and the tale of the day's deed
        could be safely kept.

I wrapped the stone in the fur of a white rabbit,
and placed it inside the Storyteller's Bag
        alongside the many other tales I
        would collect throughout my days.
And within the Storyteller's Bag,
the dragon's stone can still be found today.

"O-E-A . . . Yah!
What I have said is true.
And I, the Storyteller, do tell this tale."

Chapter Ten

Chapter Eleven: The Close-Ones Songbird

"Everything in nature has a hidden message; what a wonderful adventure it is to uncover each, one by one."

1669-1671—The Storyteller:

The Cherokee Messenger

Songbird,
whose long black hair
    would wave in every direction
    as it was blown by the wind,
was one of mystery and change.

Songbird was from the Bird Clan—
a messenger,
a keeper of birds
—One-Who-Collects-the-Sacred-Feathers—
And like the crows and the ravens,
the hawks and the wrens with whom she lived,
Songbird took news throughout the villages each day.

News of birth and death,
of triumph and loss,
of weddings and sacred ceremonies,
of good deeds and bad.

And if there was a song to sing,
or a drum being played,
anywhere within a day's walk,
Songbird was there adding her chant, her dance, her words,
and bringing her sacred feathers to revel in the ceremonies.

A gift was once placed on Songbird,
by a great Cherokee Beloved Woman.
A gift that she would one day be a great leader of women.
And this she will do,
when she finds her sacred path.

Each day,
as Songbird went out into the village,
and to the places the Cherokee lived
    in separate communities and dwellings
    along the great waterways
    of the southern Appalachian Mountains,
she collected feathers.

These feather quests
    became as important to Songbird

Chapter Eleven

as delivering messages to her people.
For it was with these feathers
    her people took part in their most ancient
    ceremonies and rituals.

Songbird had feathers
    from each of the many winged-creatures
—the flyers, the birds—
who came out of the cave
    on the day the son of Kanati [Ka-na-ti]—The-Lucky-Hunter,
and his wife Selu [Say-Loo]—The-Old-Woman-of-Corn,
gathered with his mystical friend
—The-Wild-Boy-Who-Came-Out-of-the-Water—
and let all the animals free from the cave.

Songbird also has feathers from the Little Sparrow,
the principle bird of the Cherokee—
The-Winged-One-Who-Is-Everywhere.

Feathers from the Turtledove—
The-One-Who-Cries-for-Acorns.

Feathers from the Swallow-Tailed Flycatcher,
who was once a Red-Horse-Fish,
until he changed his form and added his wings.

Feathers from the Whippoorwill,
who sings at night for the Little-People.

Feathers from the Quail,
used in the Cherokee Quail Dance.

Feathers from the Owl,
who is sometimes a ghost or witch or bearer of death—

beware of this bird at night.
It is said that if a little-one's eyes are bathed
        by the feather of an Owl that has been placed in water,
the child can stay awake all night,
even when he is old.

Feathers from the great Buzzard
        who helped shape The-Mountains-of-Blue-Haze,
and whose feathers,
placed above a cabin's door,
will keep witches away.

Feathers from the Great White Heron,
worn by the ball players in The-Little-Brother-of-War.

Feathers from the Wild Turkey,
used in the making of Cherokee clothing
        and the regal sacred cloaks of the Cherokee priests.

Feathers from the Redbird,
who is daughter to the sun,
and comes as a sacred visitor from the upper world,
to all who see her.

Feathers from the Martins,
who help tend the Cherokee gardens.

Feathers from the Kingfisher,
who was given his long and pointed bill
        to gig his prey—
a gift from the animal-chiefs who felt sorry for him.

Chapter Eleven

Feathers from the Crane,
who challenged the Hummingbird to a race,
to win the heart of the woman they both loved.

Feathers from the great Mythical-Hawk,
who has not been seen since Near-the-Time-of-Creation.

And feathers from the Enchanted Crows,
whose many stories have been lost,
but a few, which **I, the Storyteller, will one day tell.**

But on this day,
this memorable day in time,
I will speak of the great Eagle
    and how his sacred feathers are collected
    and used in Cherokee rituals
    from the most ancient-of-days.

"O-E-A . . . Yah!
What I have said is true.
And I, the Storyteller, do tell this tale."

In Quest of a Pretty-Feathered-Eagle

One winter's day,
the peace chief of the Kituwa village called for
    Songbird and Crowdancing to meet the elders
—one from each clan—
at the council house.

After a long speech,
and much smoking of a sacred pipe
    made by The-Fair-One,
the chief asked the young pair to go out

on a quest for a chosen eagle feather
to be used in the sacred Eagle-Dance-of-Peace.

Though eagle feathers may be collected
    from the ground at any time,
if one is to quest a living eagle,
from which to pull a feather,
this can only be done in the winter.
For if an eagle is caught at any other time,
it will bring countless misfortune upon the entire village.

For many moons there had been much peace
    between the Cherokee and their neighboring tribes
    in each of the four directions;
so there was to be held an Eagle-Dance
    to honor this peace.
And members of all the neighboring tribes
    would be invited to this great celebration.
The dance was to be held in the Cherokee Mother-Town,
just as soon as the buds-come-upon-the-trees.

After their quest for the perfect eagle feather,
Songbird would then become one of the messengers
    to visit each of the neighboring tribes
    and offer her chief's request and summoned call
    to the Eagle-Dance in Kituwa.
She would partake in both of these quests
    in the last days of the Snow-Moon
    and the early days of the Cold-Moon.

*"We will bring you the most beautiful
    and magical feather from the great
    and golden eagle that we can find
—The-Pretty-Feathered-Eagle—"*

Chapter Eleven

(This answer, Songbird and Crowdancing gave
to the chief.)

The young pair gathered with them a bundle of food
    and a special tool for digging,
a tool made with a long wooden handle and a curved
    and sharpened stone tied to its tip
    with the muscled sinew taken from a white-tailed deer.

Crowdancing also took with him
    his bow and quiver of arrows.
And in the pouch about his waist,
some remade tobacco and coloured beads.

Songbird and Crowdancing each wrapped themselves
    in robes made of a buffalo,
with the fur turned inside-out
    to keep them warm on their journey.
For they would be traveling during the Snow-Moon
    and the smell of snow was lingering
    in the air and already sitting deep upon the ground.

Songbird and Crowdancing walked high into the
    Mountain outside their village that day,
glad they had worn the
    moccasins-that-come-to-the-knees,
for as the land rose,
so did the snow,
coming up almost to the top of their legs.

On their journey they saw many animals
    who simply paid them no mind;
each seemed to know they were not the object
    of these hunters' charge.
Then they came upon a majestic deer

standing near an icy stream,
his head and great antlers held high.

Crowdancing asked the deer's permission to take his life
    so he and Songbird could use this gift
    to gather an eagle feather to be used in a talk-of-peace.
This is the way Crowdancing was taught by his uncle—
to take an animal's life without asking its permission
    would cause great sickness on the hunter
    and on his village.
The deer stayed his ground and lowered his head,
touching his antlers to the soil in consent.

Crowdancing placed his arrow's notch against the string,
drew back the arrow from his bow,
and let it fly.
The deer fell in the-place-where-he-stood.
And his spirit,
like a breath of smoke from the great buffalo's nostrils
    deep in the winter's air,
drifted upward into the sky-land.

Crowdancing lifted the deer and placed it across his back
    and he and Songbird continued their journey
    to the top of the nearest and tallest hill.
There they dug a pit
    large enough for both of them to fit snugly inside.

Then they gathered thick branches of evergreens
    to weave tightly across the top of the pit
    as a thin covering under which they could hide.
Atop this shelter they laid the body of the deer.

Songbird then made a small opening
    and the pair entered the pit,

Chapter Eleven

pulling the limbs of their doorway
    back into place above them.
Here in this dark space with thin beams of sunlight
    passing through their covered roof,
they waited . . . and prayed,
and waited . . . and prayed,
for the great eagle to join them
    and feed upon the carcass of the deer
    who had offered his life for this sacred task.

At first, the buzzard came.
But Crowdancing spoke a sacred formula
    and made him pass them by.
Then came the crows,
seven of them,
of the common type.
But Crowdancing spoke a short speech to the crows
    asking them to leave on this day and return another.

"At that time, my friend and I
    will give you an elk on which to eat.
One that is much larger than this simple deer."
This he told the crows, and this they heard.

After the crows left,
Crowdancing and Songbird heard
    a series of high-pitched whistles.
An eagle!

But this was not the eagle they were after,
this was The-White-Headed-Eagle,
The-Bald-Eagle.
And Songbird's well-trained ear could tell the difference.
This eagle came down
    and placed his long claws upon the deer

and began to pick at its flesh,
but Crowdancing spoke to the bird
      and told him this place was not safe for him to eat.
The bird flew away.

Finally, there was a high-pitched chirp,
and through the spaces in the branches,
Songbird saw the golden head
      of The-Pretty-Feathered-Eagle.
This was the eagle they sought.

Just like the first eagle,
this Golden-One-Who-Flies came down and sank
      his sharp talons into the deer,
pulling and tearing the skin with his claws
      and his long curved beak,
like a great panther kneading his prey
      and taking the tender meat into his mouth.

When she knew the time was right,
Songbird thrust her hand through the branched roof
      of the pit in which they sat
      and grabbed hold of the eagle's tail.
She held and pulled with all her strength,
for the eagle was mighty and strong.
But as he waved his wings hard
      against the earth and flew away,
Songbird pushed through the limbs and stood tall,
      two handsome feathers in her hand.
The sacred feathers of The-Pretty-Feathered-Eagle.
The feathers for which they quest.

Crowdancing was exceptionally proud
      of his friend's skill as an eagle catcher.
It was the first time he had taken part in this ceremony.

Chapter Eleven

There are some among the Cherokee
    trained as Eagle-Killers
—Those-Who-Take-the-Sacred-Birds-Life—
in order to gain the feathers of the wing
    as well as those of the tail,
both to be used for dances of war.
But Songbird had the gift of gaining the sacred feathers
    in a better way—a way of peace.

One of the sacred feathers from this day's quest,
Songbird gave to Crowdancing,
And one she returned to the peace chief
    to be used in the talks-of-peace.

Songbird then left the village for twelve moons,
traveling with her chief's invitation
    to a Grand-Eagle-Ball-Dance—
an invitation for all who would hear.

Crowdancing offered his feather to **me, the Storyteller,**
and I placed it in my Bag-of-Talk,
and there it can still be found today.

"O-E-A . . . Yah!
What I have said is true.
And I, the Storyteller, do tell this tale."

CHAPTER TWELVE:
The Close-Ones
Little-Rose

"Finding that which is lost and uncovering its story,
layer by layer,
is a part of each person's journey."

1670-71—The Storyteller and Crowdancing:

The Maker of Coloured Stones

Little-Rose, sometimes called Chair-Kee-Rose,
was the youngest of those called Close-Ones.
And her eyes would dance as she talked.
Little-Rose always smiled in a way that all who met her
    smiled as well.
Little-Rose took plants of all forms

and made many colours and dyes from their roots,
their stems, their leaves, their flowers, and their seeds.

She would brush the pulp from these dyes
    onto the inner-skins of animals
    which had been dried and stretched.

She would place her marks on standing stones,
the walls of caves,
and small rocks and shells,
using her paint or coloured rocks and carving tools
    to paint or scratch her elaborate symbols
    of the animals and crawling insects
    with whom she lived and called friends.

Little-Rose was of the Deer Clan—
Those-Who-Care-for-Animals,
Those-Who-Are-Keepers-of-Deer.
In days of old,
these deer were kept in corrals
    made of wooden posts,
and milked each day as drink for the Cherokee.

With her marks of brush or chisel or stone,
Little-Rose found ways to share her story with all to come.
But she would only place her markings,
of an animal or creature,
on skin or rock,
if the animal or creature had become her friend
    and had given her permission to create its form.

All in the Cherokee lands knew of Little-Rose
    and her sacred marks
    of The-Created-Ones-Who-Have-Life.
As some might tell stories

Chapter Twelve

and leave their mark with words,
Little-Rose left her mark and told her stories
    with her brush and her marking tools.
Little-Rose was not the first to leave her marks
    on the stone or skin,
but it was a tradition she would continue all her days.

On her many journeys into the woods and mountains,
Little-Rose had found more caves
    in which there were marks upon the walls,
then there are sleeps between the Green-Corn-Festival
    and the Festival-of-the-Great-New-Moon.

During the many days of summer moons,
Little-Rose would take Crowdancing
    and their other Close-Ones to these caves,
places hid away from common site,
where it was always cool and moist
    in pleasant disagreement with the summer's heat.

In these places,
The-Ancient-Ones had left their marks
    on the great stone walls,
since Near-the-Time-of-Creation.
Symbols of bison, and elk, and fish, and bird, and man,
waiting to be read by those who would follow.

"O-E-A . . . Yah!
What I have said is true.
And I, the Storyteller, do tell this tale."

The-Lost-Cave-of-the-Enchanted-Crows

On one memorable day
    Little-Rose was to take Crowdancing to a new cave,
one that was but a half-day's journey
    from the place where Crowdancing lived.
At this place,
Little-Rose needed Crowdancing's help
    in reading-the-stones—
for the markings told a different story
    from those she had found before.

"I will not tell you of the markings on these walls
    until you have seen them," said Little-Rose.
'Then we will add our marks to the wall,
to tell the tale of this day."

Within Little-Rose's painter's pouch
    she placed a chisel made of stone,
coloured rocks of red and yellow to make her marks,
feathers and thistle for brushes,
plants and roots of many colours,
and her mortar and pestle—
a wooden bowl and stone grinder
    in which to make her paints.
Little-Rose also brought extra coloured stones and tools
    for Crowdancing to make his marks on this day.

In Crowdancing's bag,
he placed three feathers of the crow—
one from his naming ceremony,
which was always with him;
one he had been given by Ray-of-Light—
a story for another day;
and one in which to capture the story,
as Crowdancing read from the stones.

Chapter Twelve

He also carried two coloured beads—
one black, one white;
a white cloth of animal fur;
and a pouch of remade tobacco,
to leave in the cave as an offering.

On this day, there was great heat.
It was the middle of the summer moons,
the time when the corn begins to ripen [July].
Crowdancing and Little-Rose set off
    just as the sun first hit the earth—
it was one of those summer days
    when-even-the-nights-are-not-cool.

It took Crowdancing and Little-Rose
    till the sun was high,
and to the south and east above their heads,
before they reached the cave
    of which Little-Rose had spoken.

The cave's entrance was beyond the simple-sight-of-man
    until they both came very near.
Here there was a slight odor of damp air
    being drawn from the cave's hidden opening
    and through the large bushes
    that grew to the front and to one side of the entrance.

Behind this thick hedge of mangled plants,
entering from the right side by way of a small opening,
likely made by animals,
access to the cave could be seen.
But the entryway
    reached only to the height of a man's knees,
and was covered by a large rough-cut stone,

rolled into place and guided by seven smaller stones,
that formed a shallow trough.

Crowdancing helped Little-Rose
    push the stone to the left
    and the moist air of the cave hit them with its full force,
the air being drawn by an opening
    somewhere on the other side of the grotto's walls.
The air was cold and damp and delightful
    against the sweat of their bodies.

There was a thin slice of light
    piercing from the back of the cave to the front,
hitting their eyes and making them squint.
But all outside this narrow ray of light,
was in darkness.

They sat in place for a few moments,
looking into the dark space,
allowing their eyes to adapt.

Little-Rose then led the way inside on hands and knees;
Crowdancing followed.
The only audible sounds were the echos of dripping water
    and a gentle whisper of wind,
offering a soft whistle for their ears.

Once inside the doorway,
the cave opened up to a tall but narrow passage
    in which they both could stand,
not side by side,
but one behind the other.

Chapter Twelve

After four small steps,
the space opened into an enormous circular chamber,
the width of four Houses-That-Are-Square,
but many hands taller.

They could now clearly see the small opening
    at the back of the chamber,
through which the beam of light had first shone
    to meet their gaze.

"This is a place of wonder, Little-Rose,"
said Crowdancing.

*"Ah, but you have not yet seen
    what I am here to show you,"*
said Little-Rose in return.

Little-Rose then took his hand
    and pointed it to the walls
And as his eyes adjusted further to the dark space,
there,
on the bouldered-rock of the cave's innermost chamber,
was the most magnificent story of crows
    that Crowdancing had ever seen.
Each crow symbol carved deep into the wall's surface,
telling its story From-Near-the-Beginning-of-Time;
each drawing telling a tale
    of light and earth and crow and beast;
images moving from right to left,
as if they if they were coming to life;
images covering all of the inner-chamber's walls,
    like the tattooing of a Cherokee warrior's body.

As Crowdancing's eyes spanned the room,
he saw that the space was not simply round,

as he had thought,
but shaped with seven definitive sides,
like the great and ancient council house of Kituwa.

Little-Rose had discovered,
The-Lost-Cave-of-the-Enchanted-Crows—
the grotto the medicine man had told Crowdancing about
     in his first days of training.
This was a place thought to have vanished from time.
The place where the true tale of the earth's beginning
     is forever told,
by an ancient clan of enchanted crows.
And where the many stories of the enchanted crows,
sent as messengers to the Cherokee people
     and those who came after them,
had long been sealed.

As Crowdancing examined each drawing,
it was as if the eyes of each crow followed him,
speaking directly to his spirit,
as he moved about the room,
as he decrypted each story laid out before him.
Each drawing spoke its tale,
with words as true as any language spoke aloud.

Among all the animals Crowdancing lived with—
deer and bison,
bear and boar,
fish and frog,
turkey and eagle,
rabbit and squirrel,
and too many other creatures to speak of—
young Crowdancing always held
     a special kinship with the crow.
This, Little-Rose knew;
it is why she had asked Crowdancing to come with her

Chapter Twelve

to see the cave first,
and be the one to tell its long-hidden tale.
And this is the speech Crowdancing spoke that day,
with Little-Rose there to hear his words,
and the Storyteller's Bag to collect his speech.
And I, the Storyteller, do tell this tell.

The First Wall: The-Days-of-Creation

As Crowdancing began
    to touch the marks on the first wall,
he began to speak,
but with a different voice,
an ancient voice,
an energy that came from deep within his very soul.
He spoke with the voice of The-Immortal-Ones.

"These first seven markings," he began,
"speak of the crow's beginning in
    The-Days-of-Creation.

"At that time there was only the place where
    The-One-Who-Is-Three
—The-Elder-Fires-Above, The-One-Who-Creates—
lived.

"The markings on the wall call this Mighty-One
    by all of these names.
But this marking at the end,
says that His true name,
His forever name,
is Ye-HO-Waah—The-Creator, The-Being-One.
For He has always been,
And will always be.

*"And just beyond a thin and sacred veil
     where Ye-HO-Waah lived,
there was a dimension
     where the sacred waters of the deep,
and all of the hidden land
     that would come from the deep,
were in darkness.*

*"This darkness was like a great mother's womb,
the womb of creation from which all the earth
     and its bounty rose up,
as The-One-Who-Is-Three,
spoke them into being,
as The Creator's Spirit-Breath went out,
and all things were formed.*

*"The-Elder-Fires-Above,
did not like the darkness
     in this place into which they looked,
so* **on the day that is called One,**
*they spoke their speech
     and made a light come forth from themselves,
and called this light Day;
and the darkness,
that was there before the beginning,
was spread apart from this light,
and this darkness,
was called Night.
There was not yet a sun or moon.
This light came from the Creator.*

"On the day that is called Two,
*The-One-Who-Is-Three spoke again,
and with His words He pushed some
     of the sacred water from the deep
     into The-Place-Above,*

Chapter Twelve

and He left some of the sacred water
in The-Place-Below.

"The-Place-Above,
He called the heavens—
this is the place of the clouds and the sky.
This is not the Creator's space.
His space is just beyond
The-Space-That-Flows-Between,
It is not a faraway place above the sky,
it is but another space that is here,
near-with-all-that-is.

"On the day that is called Three,
The-One-Who-Creates spoke a speech,
and made the earth push up
and out from the sacred water below,
so there was both land and water, soil and sea—
all just below the clouds and sky above.

"This Creator asked the new soil
to bring out many plants and fruit and trees,
all for the Cherokee to eat
and from which to make their paints.
And it was so. And it was good.

"On the day that is called Four,
The One-Who-Is-Three made two great luminaries—
one luminary to live in the day—
this one . . . he was called Sun;
and one who lives in the night—
this one . . . she was called Moon.

"The sun and the moon were made
to oversee the light and the darkness,

and they were in love.
But this love could not be,
for they could only touch their hands,
or share a kiss, once each night-day,
and again each day-night."
Crowdancing continued,
"The markings say
    that if the Cherokee rise to a bright and full sun,
or go into the night with a bright and full moon,
it is a kiss between the sun and moon.

"But, if it is a small moon at night,
or if there are many clouds in day,
it is but a touch of their hands,
a kiss is not shared.

"This sun and moon were also made
    to be signs for the Cherokee's
    many sacred festivals,
and both sun and moon
    were made to bring their enchantment
    to all who see them.

"The Creator then made many stars
    to keep the sun and moon company.
And it was so. And it was good.

"On the day that is called Five,
The One-Who-Creates made the crow
    and all his brothers and sisters
—the-flyers, the-winged-ones—
and He also made the fish,
and the monsters that live in the sea.

Chapter Twelve

*"In the beginning the fish and the flyers
    would play together all day,
they were brothers and sisters in all ways.
And it was so. And it was good.*

"On the day that is called Six,
*The-One-Who-Is-Three-Above
    made the beasts that walk on the land
    and all the things that crawl on the earth,
The-Wild-Ones and The-Ones-Who-Are-Tame.*

*"In these days,
    the beasts and the birds and the fish
    all played together,
as Close-Ones.
They also communed
    with all the plants and trees and fruit.
And it was so. And it was good.*

*"On the day that was Six,
The-Elder-Fires-Above made
    the first of the human-ones,
and called this one—Son-of-the-Red-Earth;
for he was formed from the earth's womb and soil.*

*"The Elder-Fires also made
    the one called Mother-of-All-Living-Ones;
the first woman,
and her beauty surpassed that of the first man.*

*"All the Cherokee people
    come from these two first living ones,
and all the other humans who walk and sit
    on The-Land-Where-We-Stand
    came from them as well.*

Some would be good and do good things,
and some would become bad and do bad things.
It was a choice
    the Creator gave to each of His human-ones.

"To these living ones,
The-One-Who-Is-Three-Above
    gave a part of Himself,
something that will live forever.
He breathed into them a sacred breath
—a spirit, created by the breath of His Spirit—
and these humans became talking-souls.
They bore their Maker's-Image
    and were called-on to continue this role
    all of their days.
They were to reflect, like the waters,
the image of their Creator out to the new world
    in what they both said and what they did,
and they were to bring
    the praise of the created world back to the Creator
    as a gift.

"To all the animals and all the life in His creation,
The-One-Who-Creates gave this breath,
their spirit was formed,
and they became souls.
But only to the ones He called humans,
did he give a talking-soul.

"The Creator also gave these humans,
these People-of-the-Earth,
the role of taking care of All-That-Was-Made,
and this,
some will do,
and some will not.

Chapter Twelve

"In the beginning,
these humans and animals and plants and trees
*   played together as one.*
And it was so.
It was as it should be.
And it was very, very good.

"On the day that is called Seven,
The-One-Who-Creates,
came and lived with all of His creation.
He took His place with all He had made.
The thin-space was removed
*   and the heavens and the earth were as one.*
And each day the Creator walked and talked and played
*   with all that He had created—*
a special time spent in the cool of each evening,
with the ones He called human.

"These seven days were good . . . they were not bad.

"O-E-A . . . Yah!
What I have said is true.
This is what these first seven markings tell me.
And, I, Crowdancing, do tell this tale."
(These are the words, I, the Storyteller,
heard Crowdancing speak on this day.)

Crowdancing then proceeded
        to read the other markings on the other six walls
        and this is what he said.

The Second Wall: The-Great-Deceiver

"The markings on this second wall,
tell me that these people from the Day-of-Creation
lived in peace with the crows and the beasts
and the fish and the creeping ones,
but then an enemy came to all the things that were made
and they no longer followed
The-One-Who-Lives-Through-the-Clouds,
They no longer chose to bear the Great-One's image.
They chose to follow after an enemy—The-Evil-One.
He is this one . . . this twisted mark on the wall.
It is the great snake—the deceiver.
The one with the mark of death on his back."

The Third Wall: The-Days-of-War-and-Death-and-Evil

"The markings on the third wall tell me
that after this time,
this first man and woman were sent out of the beautiful
garden in which they lived,
and a great time of war and death and evil came
upon the whole face of the earth.

"Between this world and the world above
—the human-ones' place and the Creator's-Place—
The-One-Who-Is-Three placed the veil that he had removed when He
created the earth,
back into place.
And He created A-Space-That-Flows-Between
the two spaces—
a sacred-space in which the humans could
still connect with the spirit-forms of all that lived and in which
they could meet and talk and sing and pray with the Creator.

Chapter Twelve

"Over a long period of time,
war and death and evil became so bad that the Creator
      decided to destroy all that He had made.

"He would release all the waters from below the earth,
and all the waters stored above the sky,
up-onto, and down-onto,
the earth.
And this He did!

"Only a few of the human-ones
—those who still followed the Creator's way—
and pairs and groups
      of all the beasts and birds and creeping ones,
were rescued—
saved in a huge wooden boat,
built by a prophet,
with a mighty talking-soul.
And this great flood is why,
in the land beneath the soil
      of the Cherokee Mother-Town,
and all about the soil in all the other lands,
there are still shells and shapes and forms
      that come only from the sea,
and can still be found today.

"At the time of this vast flood, and thereafter,
there were enchanted flyers,
selected from among the crows.
These flyers became messengers
      between The-Space-of-the-Creator
      and The-Place-Where-We-Stand—
into The-Space-That-Flows-Between.

"The first was of the Raven Clan,
who was released from the floating ark,
to lead the boat's crew to dry land.
And as human-ones began to refill the earth,
more and more enchanted-ones were needed.

"These enchanted crows
    were given the power to guide
    those who had lost their way,
those who were hurt or in pain,
and those who wished to once again connect
    with their Creator and His creation,
into The-Space-That-Flows-Between.

"It is in this sacred-space
    that the human-ones can now commune
    with The-Elder-Fires-Above,
and it is here they can commune
    with other spirits who-still-have-life.
It is in this sacred-space that the spirit-breath
    and talking-souls of the human-ones,
and the spirit-breath and souls of all that has life
—bird and beast and river and tree and mountain—
come out to play once again,
as they did in the beginning of time.
And it is here that the Creator of all that lives,
joins in the games, and work, and play.

"All these plants and animals and creeping ones
    were given the power
    to offer their enchantment as well;
to help the humans enter through the Thin-Spaces
    that exist within all the land.

Chapter Twelve

The Thin-Spaces
that lead to the continual flow
of The-Space-That-Flows-Between.
But the crows
—those who are enchanted—
were given a special gift as messengers
into this Sacred-Space.

"And look at this special marking on the wall!
Do you see this one, Little-Rose?
It is different from the others.
It tells that One of the Elder-Fires came down
into The-Place-Where-We-Stand
and He lived among the human-ones,
as a human.
He came to talk and do and show the human-ones
how to become as they once were,
in the beginning of time.

"This Elder-Fire was the Anointed-One,
who told the human-ones how to
be-put-back into the Creator's image.
He also told the human-ones how
to put-the-creation-back to the right,
as it should be,
as it can be once more.

"These Elder-Fires-Above say that one day they
will make the old-creation, new.
A new-creation in which the human-ones
—the talking-souls—
those who talk and do as they were first-made,
will once again be at peace with their Creator,
and all the Creator has made.
These Remade-Souls,
with their Remade-Bodies,

will live as one,
as it should have been,
as it was meant to be."

The Fourth Wall: The-Feathers-of-the-Sacred-Crow

"These markings on the fourth wall,"
Crowdancing continued,
"tell me that the crow, like the eagle,
the Cherokee are not to hunt for food,
but are to only take his life,
or his feathers,
for our sacred ceremonies.

"Some of these feathers
 are always to be left behind by the elders
 of each village as they pass from this life,
and handed down to a new one
 who is to be a Keeper-of-Feathers,
so the Crow-Dance can forever last.

"If these feathers are not handed down,
the stories of the Cherokee crow traditions
 will pass away,
and the stories on these walls will stop being told.
This is why there are so few stories of the crow in our tales."

The Fifth Wall: The-Keeper-of-Feathers

"The markings on this fifth wall,
tell me that a young one among the Cherokee
 will become a beloved-man,
a Keeper-of-Feathers,
and this task he will know before he can walk.

Chapter Twelve

This Keeper-of-Crow-Feathers
    is to keep his first feather in a pouch
    about his waist or back,
or hanging from his hair.
It is a gift from the spirit-world
    and will help show him his ways.
He will become a medicine-man
    and messenger among the Cherokee,
and to a land across the sea—
the land of his father.
But as a messenger,
he will be made different from those around him.
This is a mystery yet to be told.

"This Keeper-of-Feathers
    is to keep his stories in a Storyteller's Bag.
And this Bundle-of-Talk
    will be held by his eternal companion,
His talking-soul, The Storyteller."

The Sixth Wall: The-Seven-Crow-Clans

"These marks on the sixth wall,
tell me that the crows and the ravens
    were once of the same tribe,
but of different clans.

"As the Cherokee have seven clans,
so do the crows—fourteen clans together.
There are seven forms of crows here on this wall.
And these markings tell a story that the seven
    crow clans are the most gifted of all the flyers.
Of these seven clans,
I will now speak.

*"**The first marking of the Crow-Who-Is-Big,**
is of the Raven Clan—the great crow in the story
        of the flood.
The Raven is the largest of the crows.
Those of this clan have heads and bodies
        with great mass.
They are the strongest of the crows.
Their beaks are long and heavy and crooked;
their feathers always jagged,
looking as if they have come from a battle.
Those of the Raven Clan are warriors and storytellers.
They tell of times of great war and great pain.
The Raven comes to remind the human-ones
        to beware of entering wars that cannot be won,
or battles that have no meaning.*

*"**The second crow is the Black-Crow.**
The Black-Crows are the crows most commonly seen
        in the land of the Cherokee.
Those of the Black-Crow Clan
        are smaller than the Raven Clan.
The Black-Crows have feathers
        that are smooth and majestic.
They strut with these feathers
        and shake with their entire bodies
        like those of the Long-Hair Clan of the Cherokee.
Their beak is curved and strong.
The Black-Crow Clan is a peaceful clan.
They are helpers and messengers
        of the sacred Space-That-Flows-Between.
The Black-Crows
        have the most magic of all the crow clans,
especially when they take on the colour and form
        of a White-Crow.
In this form they can lead those within their view
        into a land of magic.
As crows of black or crows of white,*

Chapter Twelve

these, of the Black-Crow Clan,
are the most enchanted of all the flyers.
It is always good to listen and follow the signs of the
    enchanted flyers of the Black-Crow Clan,
but one must learn to distinguish the common ones
    from those that are enchanted,
for each serves a different purpose.

"The third crow is the Hooded-Crow—
of the Grey-Crow Clan.
The Hooded-Crow is the size of a Black-Crow,
but he has white on his breast
    and white atop of his wings.
Those of the Hooded-Crow Clan
    are helpers like the Black-Crows
    and sometimes appear as White-Crows,
just like their brothers of the Black-Crow Clan,
The Hooded-Crows love to hide their food,
much like the squirrel,
but will share their spoils, in times of need,
with man or beast.
Like the Little-People,
    you will sometimes find their gifts
        when least expected, but much needed.
And you will sometimes have them lead you
    into a land of unseen magic,
another trait of their Black-Crow brothers.

"The forth crow is the Rook.
The Rook has a face and beak that are white.
He has feathers that are rough and battled
    like the Raven.
But those of the Rook Clan
    are smaller than Black-Crows and the Raven.
The Rook's feathers are long and hang loose,
and their bellies are big

like the Nigh-Tanka-Okolakiciye—
the Big-Belly-Society of the Lakota.
Those of the Rook Clan are tricksters,
often in fun—sometimes in mischief.
They love to dance together in the sky,
swaying and twirling and spinning and dropping;
all doing the same dance,
as if they are one large and magical flyer.
They are here to remind the human-ones to always
hold their sacred dance ceremonies.

"The fifth crow is the Jackdaw.
Those of this clan are much smaller
than the Black-Crow.
The Jackdaw-Crows have a short beak,
a blackened forehead,
a grey neck,
and white eyes.
Those of the Jackdaw Clan often live with the faeries
and the Little-People,
in great faerie circles made of
land and trees and grass and gardens and stone,
land that may or may not be seen
from outside their realm.
But they have also learned of the Holy Places
made by humans,
and may be seen or unseen
at these sacred-places as well.
If you see a large flock of Jackdaws
flying in a united dance together,
you are near something sacred.
You may be able to enter their space,
and experience their magic,
but you must first ask their permission.

Chapter Twelve

"The sixth crow is the Chough (Chow).
Those of the Chough Clan have black bodies.
but there is a marking of ruddy-red on their beak,
and their legs and feet are ruddy-red as well.
Those of the Chough Clan are often found frolicking
*   near the sea and mountain cliffs.*
They are there to remind the human-ones that the water
*   and mountains are given as holy places,*
places for rest and for peace,
but they are also places of great power
*   and must be respected.*

"The seventh and final crow is the Magpie.
Those of the Magpie Clan
*   are like a small Hooded Crow,*
but their tail is long and thin.
The Magpie is smaller than the Black-Crow,
but his tail makes him look like he is long.
Those of the Magpie Clan
*   collect things that seem to have little use,*
but hold great magic.
If you see where a Magpie holds his treasures,
you are near the entrance of a thin-space.
You may enter this space and experience its magic,
but do not steal the holy objects,
unless the Magpie brings them to you as a gift.

"These are the clans of the seven crows.
Of each clan there will be Enchanted-Ones,
and there will be Those-Who-Are-Common.
Follow the first and there is great magic.
Follow the second and you may become lost,
even in a place you know well.
The Cherokee are called to learn the difference."

The Seventh Wall: The-Common-Crows

"The marking on the seventh wall,
the last wall,
tell me there are many
*   who will judge the Crow Clans wrongly,*
saying that all are tricksters;
that they bring omens of bad things to come;
that they are messengers of death.
But those who speak-this-speech
*   do not tell the truth . . . they tell a lie,*
O-E-A, Yah!

"The crows of which they speak
*   are the common crows,*
and not the ones who are enchanted.

"The enchanted crows are messengers-of-life;
they are ones who herald
*   The-Space-That-Flows-Between.*

"These markings tell me that many
*   ancient tales and myths and legends will be told*
—stories from many lands—
that speak of crows at places
*   of battle and pain and death.*
This much is true, it is not a lie.
But the Enchanted-Crows
*   are not at these places to tell of death,*
or to bring death;
they are there to speak of The-Space-That-Is-Thin;
they are there to guide those in pain,
into this Sacred-Space,
into The-Space-That-Flows-Between.
"This is what these seven walls tells me of the crows
*   and of the Days-of-Creation.*

Chapter Twelve

"O-E-A . . . Yah!
What I have said is true.
And I, Crowdancing, do tell this tale."
(These are the words I, the Storyteller,
heard Crowdancing speak on this day.)

Crowdancing then handed **me, the Storyteller,**
one of the crow feathers from his bag—
The feather into which his story had just been told.
I placed the feather into my Storyteller's Bag,
and within this bag it remains today.

Upon hearing Crowdancing's tale
    of the markings on the wall,
Little-Rose handed him a piece of the coloured stones,
to add his tale to what was already marked on the wall.
This he did.
But I, the Storyteller, will tell of this tale,
and more of the Enchanted-Crows,
on another day.

"O-E-A . . . Yah!
What I have said is true.
And I, the Storyteller, do tell this tale."

There were many others
    with whom Crowdancing lived and played
    in his days-of-youth,
but these I speak of today
    were those who knew him well.
These were the ones
    who shared his grand adventures
    in his youthful days-of-fun-and-folly—
The-Fair-One,
Kween,

Eoin,
Songbird,
and Little-Rose.
These were the ones Crowdancing called Close-Ones.

Chapter Twelve

Chapter Thirteen:
Beyond the Days of Fun and Folly

"There are calls that sing out to each of us
as we go through life.
But we must have eyes to see and ears to hear
or they will gently pass us by—again and again.
Do not, however,
be deceived by the ears and eyes of the mortal flesh.
For the truest calls
are made know to the eyes and ears of the soul.
They are calls into enchantment,
far beyond mere fun and folly."

The Call of the White-Crow

In the late spring,
the days of planting, 1671,
Crowdancing's father once again
     heard the sound of the White-Crow.
The sound that had mysteriously called him
     out of the mountains on the day Crowdancing was born.
A memory he had not recalled but once since that day.
It was the same pleading kraaas,
but this time,
calling him into-the-mountains,
instead of outward-home.

As he looked from the door of his cabin,
there in a tree-that-is-forever-green,
a tree standing tall to the north and west of the home,
stood the same White-Crow,
swaying and shaking-about
     on a limb that was much too small to hold his weight.
Seaspar saw and heard this crow,
not only with the eyes and ears of his flesh,
but with the eyes and ears of his very soul.

Seaspar then called to his family.
To his wife, The-One-Who-Is-Born-at-Night,
his son, Airell,
his daughter, Derdriu,
and lastly to Crowdancing, his middle son.
He asked them each to look and to listen.
And this they did.

Chapter Thirteen

"It is he," said Seaspar.
"The one who called me home."

Crowdancing knew at once of what he spoke.
And his family, soon thereafter.

"He is calling us all,
and we must go." Seaspar said.

No one could resist the call;
so they each walked as one toward the pleading kraaas,
no thought of coat or pack or food or tool.
Only what they carried with them in their hands,
did they take with them.
They simply walked.

As they stood beneath the tree
    where the White-Crow spoke and shook,
it was like a thin-veil was being lifted,
through which they each moved
    as if carried by the gentle breeze.

There was the briefest moment of intense light,
as if the sun was bursting through . . .
And they were at another place.
And "of" this other place,
and "in" this other place,
I, the Storyteller, do tell this tale.

Somehow,
Crowdancing knew this other-place at once.
He had seen it in a dream,
in a day-vision where he had flown
    as a Hooded-Crow high above the land.

And there below him,
in his dream,
had been an immense ring of trees in every shade of color.
A thick forest surrounding an ancient circular stone wall
    within which stood a village
    with an expansive sanctuary of open-space—
wondrous gardens,
grand leas of grain,
homes made of wood,
a sacred house of stone,
a holy well,
and a small group of people from many lands,
who all seemed to live and work as one.

In his vision,
there was also a gentle flow
    of the clearest water he had ever seen,
a beautiful stream
    running through the middle of the village
    from south to north,
and a pathway of stone running from east to west.
All, as seen from above,
forming the shape of the great medicine-wheel
    with each of its four directions marked
    by an individually carved story-stone—
story-stones towering tall
    at each of the four cardinal points.

And in this vision,
in this most-grand vision,
there was a Girl-in-a-Blue-Dress—
a dress spun from the stems of wild blue flax
    into linen cloth;
cloth spun on a wheel made of wood
    and woven into its form
    on a weaving loom with heavy weights

Chapter Thirteen

that hung from long strands of rope and twine;
the dress dyed to a gentle-blue
—like the sky above—
from the flowers that hung from the same stemmed flax
    from which the dress was made.
This place,
the girl, the wheel, the loom, the stream, the trees . . .
Crowdancing had seen them all,
in his vision,
in his dream.

Crowdancing and his family now moved forward
    beyond the no-longer-visible veil
    through which they had just passed,
stepping down onto the ground from a circular wall
    made of meticulously stacked stones from days of old.
A wall,
exactly like the one in his vision,
with one singular stone standing tall
    at the place where the veil had just been lifted . . .
then faded away.

The wall of stones, itself,
reached to about the height of a man's waist,
flat along its top,
and spread in a circular form outward
    as far as one could see in any direction.
And the wall encased a huge expanse of space
    that was completely surrounded,
from behind the wall,
by a thick and outward flowing layer after layer
    of trees and bushes that appeared as a solid fortress
    of wood and brush.
The stone wall and the trees outlined,
in a perfectly circular pattern,
the entire village contained within.

Crowdancing,
along with his family,
then began their slow walk toward the centre of the grand
    circular village that seemed to sit peacefully hidden
    within the midst of a large and beautiful valley
    within the Cumberland Mountains in the Valley-of-Elk.

For the land on which this village stood
    was a land long known for its majestic elk,
who forever pranced up and down its wide creek,
as it flowed from south to north.

The land around and within which this mystical village stood
    would one day be given the new name of Jellico—
called-as-such for the wild Angelica roots
    that grew alongside its waterways—
the name Angelica, with time,
shortened to Gellico,
then the spelling changed to Jellico,
as it was formed into written words
    and became the forever name
    for both the valley and village.

The Angelica plants and roots
    had long been used
    by the Cherokee, the Little-People, and the faeries,
to make a healing tonic and tea.
But at this time,
the time of this story,
the village was simply called the Village-of-Angelica,
in the Valley-of-Elk.
Crowdancing's family walked a long path
    laid deep with stone.
A path that ran from east to west,
leading toward an inner circle of open-space,
a space that was barely visible to their naked eye

Chapter Thirteen

from the far distance of the wall,
but came more and more into their view as they walked.

Great flocks of Jackdaw-Crows swarmed
    in a united dance above the family's heads,
each offering their sacred-permission to enter the space.
And to each side of their path
    were great leas of grass and grain,
of wheat and barley,
and other grains unknown to them till this day.
The wheat and barley varied from its shades of vivid green
—with more growth yet to come—
to shades of golden-brown and sun-dried—
looking to be ripe,
and ready for harvest.

As they came nearer the centre of the open-space,
a place where stood the sacred holy well
    of Crowdancing's dream,
folks of about forty in number
—people of Irish, Scottish, English, and Cherokee decent,
and some folk with blackened-copper-skin,
others with a dark-skin-mix of a mysterious race—
came outward from a great stone building,
to greet them.

But even more unique
    than this cultural mix of people,
was that among them,
and visible to everyone's eyes,
were Little-People,
like those of the Cherokee.
People who rose to about the height of one's knee,
with their hair shining black or gray
    and hanging downward to the ground.
And next to the Little-People,

were the tiniest of faeries Crowdancing had ever seen,
or perhaps he had only-ever-seen, in his dreams.

The villagers,
both tall and small,
soon began to gather around Crowdancing's family,
forming a circle of people surrounding the holy well,
some of the older ones speaking directly to Seaspar,
as if they knew him well.

"Where've ye been?" they asked, it seemed as one.
*"We've been worried something fierce since
    that day ye left.
What's it been?
Ten winters back?
It was so cold and the land so heavy with snow
    that day.
With only a few deep footprints in the snow,
that seemed to disappear into nothing,
we had no way to follow.
We all believed ye had been taken up to heaven,
on the snowy clouds."*

At once,
Seaspar's memory was recalled-in-full,
as he remembered this very place,
the place he had come when he was lost in the mountains,
those many years back.
And here,
standing before him on this day-in-time,
were many of the same folks
    who had cared for him back then.
And among them,
but now growing tall,
were those who when last seen,
were young and small.

Chapter Thirteen

Crowdancing's family then followed the villagers,
as they talked and walked,
back toward the large building
    from where they had just come.
A building behind which the sun was beginning to sit.
A building made almost entirely of stones.
Stones stacked tightly atop one another
    and packed between with waddle and dab.
A building that went straight upward
    beyond the height of two tall men, on all four sides,
then ever so slightly angled,
inward toward the centre,
so that the stones from one side of the structure,
finally came together to rest and support the stones
    from the other side,
forming a tightly packed angled roof at its peak,
which was then covered
    with a thin plaster of mud and thatch,
anywhere that rain might flow into its inner space.

The building had a massive doorway,
opening at the front and facing the east
—the direction from which Crowdancing's family had come—
a grand door made of red cedar
    through which the tallest man could walk
    standing upward with ease.
There were two small window openings
    on each side of the building
    that allowed light to enter the space,
each holding wooden shutters
    to be pulled tightly closed
against winter's cold and mighty wind;
and a large window opening at the back wall
    opposite the front door for even greater light to enter—
the last of which
    was fastly fading as the day was drawing closed.

This window stood
    the width of a man holding both his arms out to his sides,
and twice as tall,
and was filled with multi-coloured glass puzzle pieces,
the likes of which Crowdancing had never seen.

Brilliant reflections of coloured-light
    still filled the inner-space,
even as the day's light grew dim.
And at the centre of the roof,
in the middle of the room,
was a circular opening,
allowing smoke to billow upward from a fire,
and outward from the building, skyward.
The fire was being tended by two of the Little-People.

Seaspar remembered his father speaking
of this pattern of sacred buildings
    back in his homeland of Ireland.
And somewhere in his memory,
was the actual sight of these stone buildings
    that he had somehow, somewhere,
seen with his own eyes—
an abbey, a church, he recalled.
A building
    used much like the great Cherokee council house;
a place where people would come
        to take part in sacred ceremonies and rituals
        held to praise their Creator.

As Seaspar remembered this village from his days-of-past,
he recalled old stone ruins,
ruins of a building that likely stood in ancient days.
Those old stone ruins
    were all that had been in place
    when Seaspar had last seen this building.

Chapter Thirteen

But now,
from those ancient ruins,
arose something quite spectacular.
Seaspar and Crowdancing
    knew at once it was a sacred-place,
a holy sanctuary.

"We have finished our church,"
one of the villagers said to Seaspar.
*"Ye were the one to help us angle the stones for the roof.
Do ye remember?"*

Yes, he thought!
"YES," he spoke aloud!
For as they stepped further inside,
more and more memory came flooding back to Seaspar;
his time here among the villagers;
a distant but strong memory of his homeland in Ireland;
a mysterious kinship of both places;
and even a memory
    of how he had come to live with the Cherokee in Kituwa—
much in the same mysterious way
    that he now came to be in the Village-of-Angelica,
in the Valley-of-Elk.

The rest of that evening,
until the late morning-moon,
everyone sat on wooden pews
    cut from huge oak logs
    that were rubbed smooth on the top
    with tools made of metal shapes and forms
    that Crowdancing had never before seen;
each pew placed at four different angles,
creating a hollow-square around the fire sat ablaze
    at the centre of the building,

with its smoke lifting upward
    to the opening in the centre of the roof.

There were also large candle stands,
each with seven stems of upward curved arms,
placed throughout the building,
with candles already being lit by the wee faeries,
just as they had entered the space.

The older folks
—the elders of the village—
sat nearest the fire,
the younger just behind.
And the faeries and Little-People
    were spread throughout,
with each of the four groups
    of faerie and folk and village fare
    facing another group across the hollow-square.
Two of the square's sides
    made up of both women and men, boys and girls;
and the other two sides made up of only men and boys.
And they all began to sing.

It was a psalm, a hymn, a sacred song.
One they had memorized
    from an old holy book of lament, languish, and love.
A book that had come to this new land
with those who sailed across the waters from Ireland.
Each person was singing with a different voice,
    with four different sounds in all,
yet all blending together.
The mournful sound of their singing,
reminded Seaspar
    of the eerie and haunting Celtic vibrations
    that come from the Scotch and Irish Pastoral Pipes,
before they held such a name,

Chapter Thirteen

or the even older Bagpipes from his homeland of Ireland.
The Irish would one day soon,
per-fect this pipe into something
    they would call an Uilleann pipe [ILL-en],
a most unique and mystical musical device
    for which the Irish would, one day soon,
become well know across all the lands.

After two songs,
led by a man standing in the middle of the hollow-square,
with much swinging of his right hand,
Seaspar was asked to introduce his family
    to the entire group.
Then each head of each household
    introduced his family, in-turn,
to Seaspar and his family.

There were present on this evening:

The McKays, of the Scottish clan of the same name—
Sir Graham McKay,
and his wife, Esheron—Lady McKay,
from the old Irish MacReely Clan,
along with their two boys and one girl.

Those of both the McKay and MacReely Clans
    were well-traveled teachers, spiritual leaders,
and the MacReelys were mixers and blenders
    of sacred herbs and flowers for medicine.
This one, Sir Graham,
had been the one standing
    in the middle of the hollow-square
    singing and swinging his hands for all to follow.
His gift to share:

a spirit-leader
    through song and psalm and hymn and history.

The Phelps Clan, of Scotch-Irish ancestry—
Joseph and LaVerne with their two sons,
Gregory and Mick McPhelps,
and one girl—Mi-Chelle ni Phelps.
This clan had always been farmers and builders
    and had helped build the great stone church
    in which they each sat on this very night.
And they had helped plant and harvest
    the grand array of gardens
    that grew and supported the entire village.

The clans of Gibb and Spann—
both clans from mixed Scottish, Irish, and English decent,
and long known as leaders, spiritual teachers,
and those who build holy buildings and sacred grounds.
The elders of these two clans
    served as teachers within the village,
and were among those who helped plan and build
    the grand church and the sacred village sphere.

Larraidh (Lar-Raid) Propheta—
a young Scottish lad and a gifted storyteller.
Larraidh had the ability to explain mystery,
and to see far into the future.
But his visions were only into the good of the future,
never into the bad.

The Lay Family—
long born of these Mountains-of-Blue-Haze,
had many girls of beauty,
and a young lad as well.
One girl, with the name of Pretty-One

Chapter Thirteen

—though they were all pretty to look upon—
would become a great friend of Crowdancing's brother, Airell.

Painted-Warrior—
of the Long-Hair Clan of the Cherokee,
was the son of The-One-Who-Is-Born-at-Night's
    youngest brother.

Painted-Warrior was a Cartier,
through and through—
though his mother's mum was of English fare.
In their days-of-England,
    the family had made harnesses
    to connect horses to carts and wagons.
And they carried forward this skill
    among the Cherokee Cartiers of their home village.

Painted-Warrior had been away from his family
    for many moons now—
for they were back in a village very near to Kituwa,
the village from where Crowdancing and his family
    had just mysteriously traveled.

Painted-Warrior had been on a vision quest
    when he had secretly come upon the village
    through one of the underground tunnels
    that travels from just outside the great-wood,
to just inside the edge of the village,
very near its gardens behind the church.

Though young
—only one year apart from Crowdancing
    and both born under the same winter moon—
Painted-Warrior had received his forever name
    as both a Cherokee warrior and a trapper.

For he had already traveled with the Red-Chiefs into battle,
and had long trapped and traded animal skins
     with other tribes,
and with other people, from other lands,
who had now come into these mountains,
and were soon to be called Mountain-Men.
These Mountain-Men often journeyed
     through the land of the Cherokee
     to trap and trade and take wives,
wives from among the Cherokee.
This, Painted-Warrior, did not like.

I have spoken with much-ness of Painted-Warrior,
for he will soon travel with Crowdancing
     on the grandest of adventure to the land of Ireland,
but that is enough for now.
And I, the Storyteller, do tell this tale.

Black-Jack Johnson—
a lad of about the same age
     as Crowdancing and Painted-Warrior.
His skin was as dark a copper as any Cherokee in the village,
but it was said that he came from somewhere
     across the great waters.

Black-Jack was well known among the Cherokee
     for trading horses and animals hides.
He was also gifted at hiding horses
     from the Spanish and English and other intruders
     who came into the land of the Cherokee
     to take what was not theirs.
For this skill,
the Cherokee called Black-Jack,
He-Hides-Horses.

Chapter Thirteen

But the family and clan that Crowdancing
     would most and forever remember,
was the **Rose Clan**, of both Cherokee and Scottish decent—
William Rose and his wife Delphia Mae;
a boy, name of Will McRose—
the son of his father in name and clan;
and nine girls
—one in a blue dress—
whose name was Mharie,
Mharie ni Rose.
She had stood just to the left
     of the door of the stone church,
alongside her sister Catriona,
as they had each entered,
the other sisters and brother and father and mum,
scattered among the crowd.
The-Girl-in-the-Blue-Dress . . .
was the girl from Crowdancing's dream.

There were several others
     of Cherokee and Irish and Scottish and English decent
     who introduced themselves that night;
as well as those with dark skin who were not Cherokee;
and even the faerie and fae and Little-People
—who were all named for plants and trees
     or grass and grain—
shared their names,
and spoke-their-gifts.

All the older ones from each clan spoke their names first,
and told a bit of who they were,
some introducing their children as well,
before each family began to take their leave,
going only a few hand-breaths away to the rear
     and either side of the church,
where stood many square homes

of log and clay and grass and thatch.
Within one of these homes
    Seaspar had stayed when he had last been in this valley,
and in this home his family would now stay
    for the time they would remain in the village.

But these stories,
of many families and many clans,
are for another time, for another day.
They are another mystery for another tale,
or perhaps many tales.
But for this tale,
I will talk of The-Girl-in-the-Blue-Dress.
And I, the Storyteller, do tell this tale.

The-Girl-in-the-Blue-Dress

From the day that Crowdancing first saw
    The-Girl-in-the-Blue-Dress,
he knew they would be forever-linked
—be they fourteen years of age,
or be they three score and four—
to speak again of their days of youthful enchantment.
And this they would do.

For on that first night,
they had sat side by side
    among one of the four groups of singers.
They had sat with a group
    of women and men and girls and boys.
And they had sung.

Though Crowdancing had never heard
    this form of song before,

Chapter Thirteen

nor did he know any of the words,
both words and form he knew at once,
as he sat next to The-Girl-in-the-Blue-Dress.
Her gift was to share
    her words and thoughts with others,
without their former-knowing.

As the sun rose on the next day,
The-Girl-in-the-Blue-Dress had arranged
    to take Crowdancing on a tour of the village.
As they met at the stone church and began their walk,
The-Girl-in-the-Blue-Dress
    told Crowdancing the history of the village—
that it was built atop an ancient faeire-fort,
a fort that was built atop another layer of time,
that was built upon another layer of even longer time.
Each layer, with its own story to tell.

"And this place-of-many-layers
    is said to hold a special magic of its own—
a magic that the outside world is not privileged to see.
A vision only for those,
who stand for a time,
within its walls."
These words The-Girl-in-the-Blue-Dress said.

As they walked and talked,
Crowdancing quickly saw that the village was built
    much like the sacred mound-of-sand,
and the great council house of the Cherokee.
But instead of meetings held within the council house
    and upon the sacred-mound-of-sand,
these villagers gathered within the great stone building
—the church—
and within the large and open space outside this building.
In these places they gathered for ceremonies—

rituals, weddings, singings, teachings, baptisms,
and more.

Just beyond the church,
at the centre of the village,
was the great holy well which stood from olden-days,
and around which Crowdancing had met the villagers
    just the day before.
The water given by a creek
    that ran both above the ground at some places,
and below the ground at others,
coming in from the south and flowing north,
filled the well as it journeyed along.
In the village,
were no pens within which the deer or horse
    were held captive,
yet each stayed inside the circle of sacred-space,
of its own will.

But as for elk and goose and bear and wolf
—animals both wild and tame—
they entered into the village
    from outside the grand stone wall that encircled the camp,
and they came and went as they pleased.

These animals had learned to enter
    through underground passageways and caves
    where the villagers stored their winter food
    and drew their Angeli-Coal for the fires.

Within the village space
    these animals were safe from the hunters
    who roamed outside in the woods and outer lands.
And though the many types of animals
    who gathered within this space

Chapter Thirteen

might be enemies outside the great stone wall,
within its space,
all of these animals
—both tame and beast—
lived peacefully together,
lying side-by-side,
and forever playing the grandest of games.

As Crowdancing and The-Girl-in-the-Blue-Dress walked
    the village-open-space,
there were but a few much-large-trees,
and a covered arbor,
to the south side of the church.
And wooden and stone tables
    were spread throughout the open-space,
and even into the gardens.

At the arbor,
all the villagers gathered each day
    to share a ritual meal together,
just as the sun hit the middle of the sky.
And at these meals,
lessons were always taught,
sometimes with words, sometimes without.
The-Girl-in-the-Blue-Dress
    told Crowdancing that these all-together-meals,
meals held each day,
had always been shared as a life-giving-ritual.
They were meant to kept the villagers
    together, in common, as one.

The village homes behind the church
    were not that different
    from the Houses-That-Are-Square of the Cherokee,
except,
the wooden beams for these homes

were made of the entire thickness of a tree,
each log laid atop the one below it.
Each log laid long-ways rather than up and down
—four logs forming a square, or a long-square.
And all the logs were cut like a dove's tail at its corner,
holding them tightly-together,
so they may never move.

Outside the space of these Houses-of-Logs
    were gardens spread out in every direction
    to the side and behind them.
Gardens of the same crops
    of squash and beans and gourds and maize
    that the Cherokee grew in Kituwa.
But they also had twisting and twirling vines of grapes
    and other fine berries
    growing near to the Houses-of-Logs.

And as Crowdancing and The-Girl-in-the-Blue-Dress walked
    to the north, the south, and the east,
from the village centre,
they passed through the great leas of grain
    Crowdancing had seen as his family
    had entered the village the day before.

It was here among these fields
    that Crowdancing
    and The-Girl-in-the-Blue-Dress would walk,
hand-in-hand along the stone pathways
    between the fields grown high
    with wheat and barley—
fields gently waving in the breeze
    and every bit as beautiful as the leas of grass
    that stand and sway beneath the grandest Rock in Ireland
—The Irish Rock of Dunamase—
in the homeland of Crowdancing's father's clan.

Chapter Thirteen

In the days to come,
the mystery of this enchanting place in the Valley-of-Elk,
a place held apart in time and space,
brought Crowdancing and The-Girl-in-the-Blue-Dress
    often together to talk;
to walk among the leas of grass;
to sing songs in the hollow-square within the church;
to listen to the elders
    as they taught lessons about the Creator
    out in the sunlight, or in the moonlight
    of the village arbor where tables always stood;
and to even travel afoot or ahorse,
outside the village space,
to The-Place-of-the-White-Oak,
found much higher in the mountains,
up and along a slow and winding path.
At this place
— The-Place-of-the-White-Oak—
a little church-of-wood had been built;
and at this place, this set-apart-place,
Crowdancing would try his hand and his voice
    at leading a song from the centre of the hollow-square,
and sharing his stories and adventures and gifts
    as a young boy among the Cherokee.

To The-Place-of-the-White-Oak
    Crowdancing and The-Girl-in-the-Blue-Dress
    would travel once each week
—upon the first day of each—
with the Clan Phelps and others,
as they may.

These first-day-travelers would always leave
    and reenter Angelica from one of the village tunnels
    peacefully hidden beneath the soil.
No one knew for sure who had created

these ancient and secret pathways below the ground,
but on the walls within
    were held many of the same markings
    as those upon The-Lost-Cave-of-the-Enchanted-Crows.

Each of these first-day-of-the-week outings
    would start at the stone-church in the village,
just as the sun began to rise.
Here, at this sacred-place,
Crowdancing's father became the chosen-one,
to speak and teach and preach.
The villagers soon began to call him
    with the name of Preacher—Preacher-Man,
and as his son, Crowdancing,
was soon christened Son, of the Preacher-Man.
These names would follow them both for all their days,
and in ways not yet understand,
set the paths they both would take,
and lives they both would lead,
as Holy-Men.

Many songs would be sung
    within these church walls each week,
and teaching and preaching and praying
    would usually follow.
Then the villagers
    would meet out under the arbor
    for the communal midday meal.
And on this first-day-of-the-week,
a glass of wine and a torn bit of holy-bread
    would be shared, as one,
among the whole.

After the meal,
and the breaking of holy-bread,
families, but a few,

Chapter Thirteen

would then travel to The-Place-of-the-White-Oak,
where more teaching and preaching and singing
     and praying would again take place,
before they all traveled back to their village,
just before the evening sun shadowed the close of day.

As well as their work and play each week,
at the stone-church and the church-of-wood,
Crowdancing and The-Girl-in-the-Blue-Dress
     also delightfully worked and played with the village elders
     in the making of Irish whiskey they distilled
     from barley and wheat and corn,
all grown and gathered within the village sphere,
and distilled with water in a massive copper pot;
or they worked with their hands
     in picking the choicest grapes
     from the many vines behind the church,
and making wine with the village women.
In these ways they turned
     grain and grape and water
     into bread and wine and whiskey,
which brought joy and wonder and delight
     to all the village folk and fare.

And it was in these daily ventures,
of pleasuresome work and play,
that Crowdancing and The-Girl-in-the-Blue-Dress
     found the time to learn more about each other,
about each other's families,
of each other's joys and dreams and thoughts,
as they walked and talked and worked and played,
most every day.

Everything in their life took on unfamiliar meaning
     during this time together.
A deep and rich and decisive meaning

whereby everything that was done,
whether big or small, whether work or play,
had purpose and design and form,
and everything around them,
within in the landscape they called life,
opened windows and doors and passageways
       to new and alluring enchantment.
For in this time,
even the mundane had become artful adventure.
Work was play and play was work,
they were now the same.
Crowdancing had always
       held enchantment close to his heart,
but this new enchantment was of a richer-kind.

One of Crowdancing and The-Girl-in-the-Blue Dress's
       favorite things to do on a lazy day
—when one might be had—
was to steal away
       with one of the two holy books
       held within the inner-chamber of the church.

The first book was bound together with tattered pages
       and outwardly inscribed with the words:
Tiomna Nuadh ar dTigearna agus ar Slanaighteora.
[The New Testament of our Lord and our Savior].
It was an ancient book, but in the Irish tongue,
the elders called a Bible.

The other book was a gathered-grouping of unbound pages
       with Irish words and decorative drawings.
Each page written or drawn on animal skins
       that held within their pages majestic stories
       of kings and queens, of good and bad, of joy and pain.

Chapter Thirteen

The stories from both these books,
if laid end to end,
told one continuous story that spoke of the creation
    of the world and its people, it plants, its animals,
by the one Creator God—Ye-HO-Waah;
stories about the bad and good that pulled the world apart,
and put it back together;
stories about covenants made and covenants broken;
stories about slavery and exile and escape;
stories about times of war and times of peace;
stories about songs and prayers and psalms and lament;
stories about prophecy and poetry and life and lore;
and stories about all that now lives,
being remade,
one-day,
anew.
All of these mystical stories and tales,
held in this one place,
for all eyes to see and all ears to hear.

And in the book that was bound,
it spoke about special teachers—apostles,
about special followers—disciples.
It spoke about The-People-of-a-New-Covenant,
about a Messiah, a Savior, an Anointed-One, a King
—Yeshua—
In this book the Anointed-One was called both
    the Son-of-God . . . and the Son-of-Man.
He was God . . . come to earth . . . as a man.

The stories told within these books,
were about the same Creator . . . Ye-HO-Waah,
that the Cherokee of Kituwa were taught about
    by the old ones and ancient ones of days long past.
And they were about the same one . . . the Anointed-One,

written about with signs and symbols on the ageless walls
    in The-Lost-Cave-of-the-Enchanted-Crows.

When Crowdancing and The-Girl-in-the-Blue-Dress
    took these books,
they would go into the edge of the woods,
just beyond the stone wall,
to a small and open space with seven sides,
and read from their pages,
as they listened to the crows
    dancing in the trees that surrounded them.
And one day,
without the other knowing,
they both began to copy the words from the books
    and add, to them, their drawings,
of God and man and woman,
of animals and plants and seas
—of all things created and formed—
onto old animal skins that had long been stored
    within the village tunnels from days-of-old.

All Crowdancing's days here
    with The-Girl-in-the-Blue-Dress,
were somehow different from his days
    and adventures with the Close-Ones.
He would look back at this year
    as a beautiful-mystical-blur that passed all-too-quickly.
And he knew that life would not have been the same,
no matter where it led,
without this time with The-Girl-in-the-Blue-Dress
    in the Village of Angelica.
It had set a mark upon his soul.

For in this most-delightful-of-years,
Crowdancing came to know a romantic-innocence
    in each day he spent with The-Girl-in-the-Blue-Dress;

Chapter Thirteen

no less or more joyful and fun,
or less or more enchanting,
than with the Close-Ones of his village-home;
but it was a new and purposeful enchantment,
nonetheless.
An ongoing experience of living and learning and loving
    that he had never before known.

At the end of twelve full moons
    the villagers made plans to hold a grand ceremonial dance,
a blessing ball and dance to celebrate Crowdancing
    and his family's time living in the village.
For they had truly become a part
    of these people and their ways.
The day following the dance would be the one year
—to the day—
anniversary from when they had entered this space
    as a family.

There were to be Irish bagpipes and fiddles,
and the-plans-they-were-made;
there would be bodhran [BOW-rawn] drums
    and Cherokee drums beating together,
and the-plans-they-were-made;
and there was to be a sacred and magical
    Cherokee flute made of wood,
brought out just for this special occasion.

There is an old story of a White-Buffalo
    who brought the sacred pipe to the Lakota,
and of a White-Elk
    who brought the wooden flute to the Cherokee—
these are stories for another time.
But I, the Storyteller,
have one of these flutes and one of these pipes
    deep within my Storyteller's Bag.

One day . . . one day soon,
I will tell their tale.

The dancing and the ceremonies
      and the music and the feast went long into the night,
with the full moon rising high in the sky,
and joy and enchantment were found by all.

Finally, as tiredness fell upon the village fare,
each family began to leave the music and dance
      and go back to their houses-of-logs.
Never had there been an evening as enchanting as this,
for all who came.

As Crowdancing and The-Girl-in-the-Blue-Dress
      shared their last dance and said goodnight,
they parted with a first-kiss.
How were they to know . . . it would also be their last?

The next day the villagers all stayed long in their beds.
But Crowdancing,
along with his father and mother and brother and sister,
were up and out to meet the day as the sun began to rise.
They had dipped in the holy well seven times,
then walked to the far edge of the village to pray,
and had come upon the place of the thin-veil
      from where they had entered the village
      exactly one year before.

And as they walked,
they were singing an Irish song of olden times,
but this time they were singing it
      in the new way the villagers sang.
They were singing a new-song,
with four different sounds

Chapter Thirteen

coming from the five,
making one lovely and mystical sound
    to awaken all the forms of life
    that surrounded them on this day.
Their very words and tunes
    caused each faerie-form they passed,
to rise up and out of the trees and flowers and stones
    they called their homes,
and to shake the long-night's-dust from their weary eyes.
For they had taken part in all the evening's festivities
    of fancy dress and dance, as well.

As they continued to walk and sing,
there perched on a tree-that-stays-forever-green,
appeared a White-Crow;
the same enchanted White-Crow
    they had not seen for the longest-of-time.
But he was once again,
swaying and shaking and dancing his call,
and pleading his sound,
with the deepest of kraaas.
And they each knew at once,
what it meant!
Without even the time to gather a coat or food,
or even to say goodbye to their friends
—their new family, those they now loved—
they were drawn,
once again,
into the veil and through to the other side.

There,
in only a moment of time,
they were back in their Mother-Town of Kituwa.
It was summer, 1672.

As they walked into the village,
many of their family and friends ran out to greet them.
"Where have you been?" they asked.
"It has been twelve full moons since we last saw you!"

Yet,
to Crowdancing and his family,
it seemed they had only been gone
      for a such a short amount of time.
It would only be in later years that Crowdancing
      would truly understand the mystery of the year
      he had spent in the Village of Angelica.
It had added a new level
      of mystical and meaningful enchantment
      to that which he already held
      within his eyes, his ears, his hands, his heart.
Crowdancing was forever changed.

But . . . this was not the day I spoke of
      that changed everything.
For that is next-to-come.

"O-E-A . . . Yah!
What I have said is true.
And I, the Storyteller, do tell this tale"

Chapter Thirteen

Chapter Fourteen:

Crowdancing and the Cherokee Medicine Man

"It is often hard to determine good from evil,
but that we must,
or evil will determine us."

December 7, 1672—The Storyteller:

The story is told,
and I, the Storyteller, do tell this tale,
that upon his return from the Village of Angelica,
Crowdancing advanced more quickly,
from his days of fun and folly,
and with his many gifts and talents,
far beyond what one would call ordinary.
He seemed to know things before he was told,
learn skills before he was taught,

see things before they happen,
and experience the world of nature that surrounded him
    in a manner that can only be perceived
    through mystery and enchantment.
Some of these gifts he had before,
but now . . . now they were all . . . somehow . . . new.

Just five years before this time,
Crowdancing had been easily drawn
    to the Red-Paint Clan,
to learn of the medicine-way.
Most medicine men are born into the Red-Paint Clan
    and the ways of medicine or sorcery or wizardry;
some . . . are simply drawn to these ways
    and learn the sacred formulas and ceremonial practices
    from Those-Who-Know-Much.
Crowdancing was of the latter;
his teacher . . . the former.

A forever twist in Crowdancing's tale came
    on the day of his birth—fifteen years later.
At this time,
he had spent four winters under the guidance
    of one of the great medicine men of his tribe—
He-Who-Knows-Most, of the Red-Paint Clan.
Crowdancing had studied
    with this medicine man intently
until that year he and his family
    had been drawn away by the White-Crow.
And upon his return,
he had once again resumed his studies,
though something was now different, and aloof.

The Red-Paint Clan are healers and have always been,
but some are sorcerers and witches
    and wizards and man-killers,

Chapter Fourteen

who can steal the spirit from one's body and soul
    and take him to the place of death.
These wizards and witches
    often watch over one who is ill, to bring him trouble.
They can also shoot an invisible arrow
    into someone they dislike, and make him sick.
These medicine men and wizards
    carry with them the power to conjure
    both good and evil.
Sometimes this line between medicine man and sorcerer,
is very thin and hard to know.

Whether for good or for evil,
good medicine or bad medicine,
on this specific day in time—December 7, 1672—
the Cherokee medicine man
    who had been training Crowdancing
    for these many years,
placed an ancient curse on Crowdancing's human form.
A spell that altered his life beyond imagination;
a spell that changed him,
forever,
into a koga [ko-GA];
a crow . . . nevermore a boy to be.

But not just any crow, mind you;
but an enchanted crow
    who could communicate with all the other animals
    even more so than when he was a human.
A crow who knew about the Thin-Spaces
    that exists everywhere;
that thin-veil that separates the spirit world
    from the natural world.
And he could guide those he desired through this veil,
into the Sacred-Space-That-Flows-Between;
that space where heaven and hearth meet and overlap.

A crow who also knew the Sacred-Places,
and the Thin-Places that exist within structures made by man
    and those made by The-One-Who-Is-Three.
Places that open up . . . into the forever-flow . . .
of The-Space-That-Flows-Between.

All this wisdom was given to Crowdancing
    the moment the great sorcerer shifted his shape
    from that of a human,
to the sacred-messenger form of an enchanted crow.
He would spend the rest of his life
    expanding these gifts and talents,
and advancing his newfound mystical knowledge.

The one form of communication
    the medicine man *took* from Crowdancing,
was that he could no longer speak
    the language of humans—
at least not with human words as he did when he was a boy.
He could still understand these human words,
but he now had to speak
    in ways other than that of spoken words.
For human words,
he could no longer convey.

Some say the medicine man acted that day
    because he was jealous of Crowdancing's powers—
that Crowdancing's skills had already surpassed his own.
Some place the blame on Crowdancing's absent year,
away from the medicine-man's training.
Others say that the medicine man saw something magical,
something enchanting, in Crowdancing,
that he could best render in the form of a crow—
a winged messenger of Ye-HO-Waah.
And thus, he made him so.

Chapter Fourteen

For whatever the reason,
we may never know.
For on the day that Crowdancing was transformed
    into an enchanted crow,
the medicine man vanished from his human existence,
and was never seen again.

In his newfound life as a crow,
Crowdancing discovered he also had the unique power
    to alter the colour of his feathered-cloak.
The power to change his feathers
    from that of a shimmering Black-Crow—
from the blood of his Cherokee mother;
to the feathers of a white-hooded crow—
from the blood of his Irish father;
and sometimes . . . when truly needed,
he could shift to the most mystical crow of all,
the crow that is all-in-white.

The crows of the Cherokee
    are the most beautiful-black in all the land—
a black as dark and piercing to the eyes
    as a piece of ancient coal
    dug from the peat and first brought to light.

And the Irish Hooded Crow?
Awe!
He is the grandest mix of brown or black with white.
For Crowdancing,
these Irish colours became all-white,
but for a hood of chestnut brown
    on the crown of his head
    and a softer brown
    on his outer wings and the feathers of his tail.

With as simple as a thought of either hue
—black or white—
or of either heritage
—Cherokee or Irish—
Crowdancing could shift his paint.

With the gift of enchantment
    offered by that which he experienced most every day,
in nature,
or within the mystery of a special place or time,
Crowdancing would change his colour,
and with it move from a state of mind and body,
to one of spirit and soul.
From black to white,
from white to black.

In this ethereal state
—in The-Space-That-Flows-Between—
his abilities, his skills, his talents,
were without limit.

"O-E-A . . . Yah!
What I have said is true.
And I, the Storyteller, do tell this tale."

Chapter Fourteen

Chapter Fifteen: Shifting Colours

*"Never let your memories simply become
sweet vapors of an exhausted past."*

December 8, 1672 and After—The Storyteller:

I sometimes think that Crowdancing
    was happy in this new life,
with the freedom to walk the earth,
and fly far above it.

With his gift of discerning The-Spaces-That-Are-Thin
    that guide us into The-Space-That-Flows-Between—
that space between The-Space-Through-the-Clouds,
and The-Place-Where-We-Stand.
That space that separates the-sacred from the-mundane.

With his knack for knowing the pathways
        into The-Space-That-Flows-Between—
the Sacred-Space that joins our two worlds
        and sometimes overflows with enchantment,
into the physical world of matter.

With his skill in communicating with all the animals;
and his ability to shift his colours
—the paint of his feathers—
and enter the enchanted land of mystery.
Don't we all wish for such magic . . . at least a bit!

But I know for a fact,
in this I do not lie,
and I, the Storyteller, do tell this tale,
that he also missed his life as a lad.

He yearned for those things most young boys
        took for granted—
sitting down to eat or play with his family,
taking a young girl to a dance and stealing a kiss
—just one more time—
or simply talking with his friends with common words.

In his new life,
these things were only memories,
sweet vapors of an exhausted past.
A past that was good;
a life that was grand;
a life for which he grieved.

But, Crowdancing's new life was also filled
        with unimaginable new adventures and magic.
His new life was *fully-enchanted;*
something he had glimpsed as a boy,

Chapter Fifteen

but had never fully come to know!
For true enchantment,
he was soon to find,
was far beyond any experience
    he had hitherto encountered.

While he may never dance with
    nor kiss another human-girl,
Crowdancing somehow knew
    he would find his new place,
in whatever was presented to enchant him each new day,
in big ways and in small.
He knew within his heart
    that he would find authentic magic
    in the journeys to be laid out before him.
And this he did!

"O-E-A . . . Yah!
What I have said is true.
And I, the Storyteller, do tell this tale."

Chapter Sixteen
and
Book II: Preview

Crowdancing and the Cherokee Little-People

"What we don't see is often there with us multi-fold, and what we do see is often simply a thin covering over something ethereal and beneath. Sometimes we must shut our eyes and open our heart in order to truly see."

December 8, 1672-1675—The Storyteller:

In those first few weeks of his transformed life,
Crowdancing often found himself in the early moonlight,
or just before the first break of the dawning sun,
cheerfully dancing among the Cherokee Little-People—
the illusive Indian spirit-forms
      found in the nearby woods and fields,
in the mountains and hills,
in the caves and valleys that surrounded him.

Or . . . he might be seen as he enchanted the faerie and fae,
who were from a different land
—the land of the Emerald Isle—
with his ability to shift and change his colours.
And he also delighted
      when the faeries and fae shifted and changed
      from the emotional energy of the very land
      in-which they lived,
into something almost visible, almost human.

When in his new form
      as a Cherokee Enchanted Black-Crow,
Crowdancing easily knew where the "Thin-Spaces" *were*,
and where the "Thin-Places" *were* as well.

And when he shifted into an Irish Hooded-Crow,
he could enter into this realm.

As he came near to a Thin-Space,
or a Place-That-Is-Thin,
a shift would occur.
His entire upper body,
his shoulders and head and wings,

Chapter Sixteen

would begin to quiver—or *Shake*,
as the Little-People would call it.

The Little-People then begin to speak
    of the Thin-Places themselves as *Shake*,
and this they still do today.
And if you are blessed to see a crow quiver and shake,
you are at the opening to A-Place-That-Is-Thin.

Listen with your ears and feel,
look with your eyes and smell,
touch with your hands and see.
It's all there waiting, just beyond the veil.

And there is much more to tell!
But you must wait for The Storyteller
    to open his second book,
and pull forth its stories,
from his Bundle-of-Talk,
from deep within his Storyteller's Bag.

"O-E-A . . . Yah!
What I have said is true.
And I, the Storyteller, do tell this tale."

About the Author

I've always loved crows, and in my young twenties I joined the
Young Adult Conservation Corps as a Wildlife Biologist for the
U.S. Fish & Wildlife, working with an animal damage control unit
in West Tennessee . . . studying crows, blackbirds, and other wild
animals who have been forced to make their way living alongside
us humans, who have most often invaded their space—the space of
birds, bears, deer, wild turkey, bats—to name but a few.

By training and major career experiences, I was a medical health
educator, a college president, a college and university professor, an
academic researcher and fellow, a teacher, a minister, and a writer.
My doctoral degree is in Higher Education—Sensory Teaching
and Learning—with an emphasis in Health, Wellness, and Human
Performance—how our thoughts, actions, and sensory activities
affect our well-being. And my post-graduate studies have been
on sacred-space and sacred-place, mystery, enchantment, and the
expanded-imagination.

For my dissertation research, I lived and worked on the Eastern
Band of the Cherokee Indian Reservation in Cherokee, North
Carolina—the place in and around which most of this story takes
place. Many of the traditional Cherokee stories and myths that

I share are my re-creation of what I learned while living and working on the Reservation—a place better known among the Cherokee today as the Qualla Boundary.

The Irish stories and myths and people and places were a part of my post-doctoral research as I worked in, and studied about, sacred-places and sacred-spaces in the Midlands of Ireland, in the village of Abbeyleix, County Laois—a beautiful little village nestled at the very heart of this entire trilogy, and every bit as majestic as the land of the Cherokee.

I was once told that perhaps I am a Christian mystic at heart—in that I am a Christian always in search of true-mystery. And as you read *Crowdancing and the Cherokee Storyteller's Bag,* I hope you find just a bit of that mystery revealed.

About the Author